P
Re

Jeroo

101 Parsi Recipes

Jeroo Mehta

PopulaR
prakashan
www.popularprakashan.com

POPULAR PRAKASHAN PVT. LTD.
301, Mahalaxmi Chambers
22, Bhulabhai Desai Marg
Mumbai - 400 026.

First Published 1973
First Reprint 1979
Second Reprint 1983
Third Reprint 1987
Fourth Reprint 1995
First Edition 2008

(4115)
ISBN 978-81-7991-367-3

Photography : Bharat Bhirangi

Food Preparation and Styling : Farrokh Khambatta

Typeset by Allreach Enterprises
G-8, Sumeet Sadan C.H.S.,
Bhagoji Keer Marg
Mahim, Mumbai - 400 016.

Printed in India
by Alert Packaging House Pvt. Ltd.
326, A to Z Industrial Estate
Ganpatrao Kadam Marg, Lower Parel
Mumbai 400 013.

Published by Ramdas Bhatkal
Popular Prakashan Pvt. Ltd.
301, Mahalaxmi Chambers
22, Bhulabhai Desai Marg
Mumbai - 400 026.

To Lily, my mother

My Thanks

For their enormous help to: my mother; my sisters Naju and Freny; Khorshed Kalapesi; Roshan Kalapesi; Homai Mandviwalla; Dhun Nanavati; Roshan Munsif; K. Singhal; T. S. V. Pillai; Anthony D'Souza. Also to friends who have helped with advice and suggestions.

Big thanks to my husband Dorab, for his unflagging help and encouragement during the entire period of the preparation of this book.

But my biggest thanks go to Farrokh Khambatta, owner of the famous "Joss" restaurant in Mumbai, for the food preparation and styling and for his generous offering of the use of his restaurant and valuable time.

I cannot end without a word about my children Cyrus and Khorshed, whose uninhibited appreciation of the dishes cooked during the preparation of this book made it a joy to write and offer them to others.

Cover Photograph:
Antique Silver Fish courtesy Phillips Antiques, Colaba, Mumbai.

About the Author

Jeroo Mehta, who studied Journalism at New York University, was Associate Editor of Eve's Weekly for three years. She has also contributed articles to well-known weeklies like the Illustrated Weekly of India and the Sunday Times Supplement. Her experience of cooking and entertaining, both at home and abroad, together with her fluent style of writing, makes the book particularly desirable.

Also the editor of Time-Life books requested and published some of her recipes in their famous series 'The Good Cook'.

The author has been able to select the dishes most popular with Parsis and non-Parsis alike, and the simple, detailed manner in which she has written the recipes make them easy to follow by those who already know Parsi cooking, as well as those who venture to try it for the first time.

Here is a book that will be used over and over again by the connoisseur and novice alike.

Introduction

Our Zorastrian ancestors came to India from Persia thirteen centuries ago. Over the past hundreds of years, while the Parsis have been assimilated into the varied cultural pattern of this ancient land, they have also contributed some distinctive characteristics and features to the Indian way of life. Their culinary art is one such example. Originating from the shores of the Caspian, their food, with its very special flavour, has, over the years, absorbed the exotic flavours and irresistable tastes from the kaliedescope which makes up the cooking of India—as varied, colourful and individual as its life and customs.

They have also experimented with Western flavours and introduced to their food a happy blend of East and West which makes it uniquely different.

Perhaps because of this, Parsi cooking appeals not only to people from all parts of India but also from different parts of the world. I first became aware of this while I was a student in New York. My school held a fête at which there was a stall of food from different countries; the Chicken Vindaloo which the school cook prepared from my mother's recipe disappeared in less than an hour while the stall was still well-stocked with other dishes!

During my husband's assignment abroad where we entertained people from so many different countries, it was the genuine appreciation of the fare which was served at our table that first gave me the idea of compiling a book of Parsi recipes. It was the constant persuasion of friends that made me finally do it.

The recipes in this book are traditional and representative and include many delicious ones passed down to me by my mother. The style is simple and each step has been explained in detail. For those who will cook abroad, substitutes have been suggested for ingredients not readily available there; for the busy housewife in India I have suggested short cuts with ready-made masalas and essences which are in the market.

The idea of the book is to enable well-known and well-liked Parsi recipes to gain even wider appeal, and to offer enjoyment not only in the eating, but in the cooking of them as well.

Contents

MEAT

RICE, CURRIES AND DALS

EGGS

VEGETARIAN

DESSERTS

MISCELLANEOUS

Weights and Measures

Weights of the ingredients for the recipes in this book have been given in kilograms as well as pounds. For practical purposes, and because a fraction of weight one way or another does not make a difference to the recipe, the kilogram and the gram have been converted to the nearest, and not always the exact, equivalent in pounds and ounces. The same applies for the conversion of centimeters into inches.

1 kilogram	= 2 pounds 2 ounces	112 grams	=	4 ounces
½ kilogram	= 1 pound 1 ounce	225 grams	=	8 ounces
¼ kilogram	= 8½ ounces	450 grams	=	1 pound
28 grams	= 1 ounce	2½ centimetres	=	1 inch

The American cup is used as a measure in this book.

1 cup = 225 ml or 8 liquid ounces.

Ingredients are also given in tablespoon, dessertspoon and teaspoon measures which are quick and easy to calculate. All measures are taken level.

ABBREVIATIONS
kg = kilogram

g = gram

lb = pound

oz = ounce

cm = centimeter

Hints and Suggestions

1. **Dried Red Chillies:** The best flavour and colour is provided by Kashmiri chillies or Goa chillies which are very red and quite large without being too pungent. They can be deseeded before using in case the food is not desired to be too chilli hot.

2. **Fresh Green Chillies:** The number of chillies to be used in a recipe depends on the size of the chilli. Generally speaking, the smaller the chilli the more pungent it is. The chillies may be deseeded before being chopped or ground if the food is not required to be chilli hot.

3. **Coconut Milk:** To extract milk from coconut, add to freshly grated coconut, hot water, a little less than the amount of milk required e.g. for 1 cup milk of ½ grated coconut add 1 cup less 2 tablespoons hot water. Let stand about 15 minutes then squeeze coconut, squeezing out as much milk as possible. Discard pulp and strain liquid before using.

   If more than 1 cup coconut milk is required from ½ grated coconut, it is better to soak coconut first in 1 cup hot water and squeeze out the milk. Then do not discard pulp but add as much more water as is required and repeat process. The second milk will be thinner than the first, so keep it separate and add separately while cooking.

4. **Cooking Medium:** Although vegetable oil is mentioned in all recipes, hydrogenated cooking mediums or clarified butter (ghee) may also be used. The recipes state "remove excess oil" after frying onion because onion is best fried in a generous amount of oil. This oil can be used again. Oil or ghee should not be boiling hot when ingredients are added unless specifically mentioned.

5. **Fresh Coriander:** There is no substitute for fresh coriander. It is a mistake to believe that parsley, which somewhat resembles it in looks, can be substituted for it. The two flavours are entirely different. When measuring chopped coriander the measuring cup should be lightly packed.

6. **Eggs:** Always break an egg into a bowl to see if it is good before adding to other ingredients.

7. **Masala:** Masala means a combination of spices. Often it is ground into a paste. This can be done either on the masala stone or in an electric blender. In case the blender is used, liquid such as water or coconut milk (if it is included in the ingredients of the recipe concerned) should be added. Hard ingredients like cinnamon stick should be pounded and broken up before putting into the blender, and other ingredients like chillies can be roughly chopped to quicken the process of pulverising.

8. **Garlic and Ginger:** As pods and flakes or cloves of garlic vary in size from place to place and season to season, the correct measure can only be achieved after grinding. For this reason in most recipes the measure of garlic after grinding has been indicated in brackets.

   Ginger may be cut roughly to the size mentioned in the recipe.

   A paste of garlic and ginger can be made by grinding on the masala stone or using an electric blender. If using a blender, the garlic and ginger should be roughly chopped and some water added. In a blender it is better to make a larger quantity, then store in the refrigerator in an air-tight jar, and use as required. Ready ground garlic and ground ginger on a mixture of the two are also available at food stores.

9. **Dhansak Masala:** This is a very special masala made for the rice and dal dish called Dhansak, but is also used in certain other recipes. There is no substitute for this and it should be omitted from a recipe if it is not available.

10. **Salt:** Salt seems to vary in strength according to various packings and different places. The salt mentioned in the recipes in this book is table salt. Using the measure given as approximate, it should be tried out for taste once and, if necessary, altered according to taste in successive recipes.

11. **Tamarind Juice:** Soak the tamarind pulp in required amount of hot or boiling water for 15 to 20 minutes. Then strain liquid through a fine sieve or strainer into another

container pressing down hard on the stringy tamarind to extract as much juice as possible. Discard pulp and use liquid.

12. **Pressure Cooking:** Most of the chicken, meat and dal (lentils) dishes can be cooked in a pressure cooker. The main difference will be in the amount of liquid to be added. In the pressure cooker only that much liquid is to be added as is desired for gravy so long as it is not less than the minimum amount of liquid suggested in the manual of instructions accompanying the pressure cooker.

    For cooking dal as in the recipe for "Masoor" where no gravy is required, add water in the proportion of 1 cup dal to 2 cups water.

13. **Kadai:** A kadai is a deep bowl-shaped vessel which is good for deep-frying. Instead of a kadai, deep-frying can also be done in a wok, a deep frying pan or a skillet except for puris which can only be fried in a kadai or a wok.

Substitutes

Although it is best to use the original ingredients as mentioned in the recipes, in case of difficulty in obtaining them, satisfactory alternatives are suggested below.

Milk of fresh coconut can be substituted by Cream of Coconut if cooking abroad. 55 g (about 2 oz) Cream of Coconut plus 1 cup water is equivalent to 1 cup milk of ½ fresh coconut. Unsweetened coconut powder may also be used. Add 1 cup water to 25 g coconut powder. Mix and let stand 15 minutes. Then add ½ to 1 cup more water if needed. Mix and let stand 5 minutes before using, for best flavour.

For **fresh grated coconut** when it is to be ground into a chutney or masala paste you may substitute desiccated coconut. ½ fresh grated coconut is equal to 4 tablespoons desiccated coconut.

Instead of grinding the **garlic and ginger** to a paste, the garlic may be crushed and the ginger sliced very fine. Ginger powder may be used instead of fresh ginger root if the latter is not available. The result is not quite the same but very similar.

For **dried red chillies** you may substitute chilli powder (ground hot red pepper). 4 chillies equal 1 teaspoon chilli powder.

For **coriander seeds** you may substitute coriander powder.

1 tablespoon coriander seeds equals 1 tablespoon coriander powder.

For **cumin seeds** you may substitute cumin seed powder.

1 teaspoon cumin seeds equals 1 teaspoon cumin seed powder.

For **black peppercorns** you may substitute black peppercorn powder.

For **cloves** you may substitute clove powder.

For **cinnamon stick** you may substitute cinnamon powder. 1 inch cinnamon stick is equal to ¼ teaspoon cinnamon powder.

For **tamarind pulp** you may substitute tamarind concentrate or vinegar.

1 tablespoon tamarind pulp is equal to 1 teaspoon tamarind concentrate or 1 tablespoon vinegar.

For **jaggery** you may substitute brown or white sugar.

Fish

Fish is a favourite with Parsis and many must have it daily. The rich variety of sea and river fish available in India makes it easy enough to serve it at table in so very many delicious ways.

There are some truly delectable varieties of fish which, unfortunately, are not available everywhere. For example the Pomfret, whose flavour is difficult to compare, and the Bombay Duck whose habitat is along the Western shores of India. The Indian Salmon or Rawas, is a smaller fish than the English Salmon but its tasty white flesh is particularly suited to the palate of a gourmet.

For cooking abroad, however, they can be substituted. Plaice can be used instead of Pomfret in a recipe where the fish remains whole. Instead of sliced Pomfret or Indian Salmon, slices of Halibut can be used, and for fillets of Pomfret, fillets of Sole can be substituted. The Bombay Duck, however, is unique and has no substitute.

A word of warning about cleaning fresh fish before cooking. The prawn or shrimp has a black thread-like vein which must be removed carefully and completely and the Bombay Duck has two fin-like protrusions on either side of the tail which must be taken off and the stomach should be completely cleaned. The Pomfret and Indian Salmon are cleaned by making an insertion at the neck and thoroughly cleaning out the neck cavity and the stomach.

As it is dangerous to eat fish which is not competently and thoroughly cleaned, it is advisable to learn how to do it before attempting to cook it.

1. Chutney-Stuffed Pomfret

This dish can rightly take pride of place in the book.
It is one of the most delicious and traditional
ways of serving Pomfret.

INGREDIENTS

1 large pomfret, cleaned
and kept whole

¾ teaspoon turméric powder ⎤

¾ teaspoon chilli powder ⎬ Mix together

1 teaspoon salt ⎦

1 teaspoon flour

Vegetable oil for frying

Green Chutney

¾ cup grated fresh coconut or 6 tablespoons
desiccated coconut

½ cup roughly chopped fresh coriander

3 green chillies

4 large cloves garlic

½ teaspoon cumin seeds

2 teaspoons lemon juice

½ teaspoon salt

1 teaspoon sugar

METHOD

1. Wash the fish after rubbing a little flour over it to remove any very fishy smell.

2. Apply chilli mixture to entire surface of fish and allow to marinate at least 1 hour.

3. Grind to a fine paste all chutney ingredients except lemon juice and salt. Add lemon juice and salt to paste.

4. Stuff as much of this chutney as will conveniently fit into the neck cavity of the fish. (Serve any remaining chutney separately).

5. Pour 2 or 3 tablespoons oil in "tava" or iron griddle or heavy-bottomed frying pan. Heat to sizzling hot, put fish in it, lower heat at once and fry till bottom skin of fish is nicely browned and crisp. Turn the fish and cook other side similarly.

6. Serve at once, garnished with sprigs of parsley, slices of tomato and whole boiled potatoes brushed with butter.

❑ Serves 4

2. Prawn (Shrimp) Kavabs

A tasty variation from the usual minced meat kavabs,
these can also be served as cocktail eats
if made into smaller bite-size balls.

INGREDIENTS

2 cups shelled, cleaned prawns, carefully deveined

2 medium onions, finely chopped

4 green chillies

6 cloves garlic (¾ teaspoon) ⎫ Grind to

1 teaspoon cumin seeds ⎭ a paste

2 tablespoons finely chopped fresh coriander

1 teaspoon turmeric powder

4 teaspoons lemon juice

1 egg

2 slices bread, soaked in water

2 teaspoons salt

1 cup dried breadcrumbs

Vegetable oil for frying

METHOD

1. Slightly mash prawns on masala stone or put through mincing machine.
2. Remove bread from water and squeeze dry.
3. Add to prawns all ingredients except breadcrumbs and oil. Mix thoroughly.
4. Divide mixture into 12 or 14 portions. Shape each portion into a ball.
5. In a deep frying pan or a kadai, pour oil to a depth of 4 cm (1½ inches). Heat to medium hot.
6. Roll each "ball" in breadcrumbs and fry on medium heat till nicely browned.
7. Serve as an individual dish with potato chips or potato straws (p. 67) or serve with "Dhansak" instead of meat kavabs.

❑ Serves 4

3. Kolmino Patio
Prawn (Shrimp) Patio

*Prawn or Shrimp Patio is a popular dish
when prawns are in season and
a very traditional way of cooking them.*

INGREDIENTS

1 cup (about 25) shelled
   and cleaned prawns (shrimps)

4 large cloves garlic (1 teaspoon)
4 dried red Kashmiri chillies   } Grind to
1½ teaspoons turmeric powder   a paste
¾ teaspoon cumin seeds

1 medium onion, finely sliced

3 medium onions, chopped

1½ dessertspoons finely chopped fresh
   coriander

1 cup tamarind juice of 1 tablespoon
   tamarind pulp (p. 17) or 1 teaspoon
   tamarind concentrate (p. 19)

1 tablespoon grated jaggery

1½ teaspoons salt

2 tablespoons vegetable oil

METHOD

1. In a pan heat oil, add 1 sliced onion and fry till golden brown.

2. Add masala paste and cook 5 minutes till well blended.

3. Add prawns and stir till well mixed with onion mixture.

4. Add chopped onion, coriander and salt and stir well.

5. Add ¼ cup water, cover and simmer, allowing prawns to cook in onion juice.

6. When prawns are cooked, add tamarind juice or tamarind concentrate and jaggery
   and cook a few minutes longer till jaggery has melted.

7. Serve as an individual dish, sprinkled with some chopped fresh coriander or as an
   accompaniment to White Rice (p. 77) and Mori Dal (p. 84).

❏ Serves 4

4. Fish Cutlets

This simple and tasty mixture can be made into
fish cutlets, fish kavabs or
fish rolls and decoratively served with vegetables.

INGREDIENTS

400 g (1 large 14 oz) Pomfret or other white
fleshed fish, sliced

1 medium onion cut into 2 pieces

1 teaspoon salt

1 tablespoon very finely chopped onion

1 tablespoon finely chopped fresh coriander

2 green chillies, finely chopped

2 tablespoons tomato ketchup

1 tablespoon Worcestershire Sauce

2 medium slices bread

1 large egg

½ cup dried breadcrumbs

Vegetable oil for frying

METHOD

1. Boil fish in 1 cup water with 1 teaspoon salt and 1 onion cut into 2 pieces.

2. When cooked, remove fish from pan and remove skin and bones from fish.

3. Mash the fish with a fork.

4. Soak bread in water for 10 minutes.

5. To the mashed fish, add the chopped onion, coriander and chillies. Also add tomato ketchup, Worcestershire Sauce and egg. Taste for salt.

6. Remove bread from water and squeeze dry. Add to fish mixture and blend all ingredients well.

7. Divide mixture into 10 equal portions. Roll each portion into a ball. Roll each ball in the breadcrumbs and flatten out and shape each into a cutlet.

8. Pour oil in a frying pan upto a depth of 1¼ cm (½ inch), and heat to medium hot. Fry cutlets in it till they are golden brown on both sides, turning once.

9. Serve with, mashed potato and boiled peas or with slices of Fried Brinjal (p. 124).

❑ Serves 5

Facing page—Patra-ni-Machhi (page 31),
Overleaf—Chutney-Stuffed Pomfret (page 21)

5. Luganno Sas

Fish in Spicy White Sauce

*Slices of fish cooked in a gently spiced sweet and
sour sauce and usually served at weddings.
Also a favorite served with Khichdee.*

INGREDIENTS

450 g (1 lb) Pomfret, Surmai or Indian
Salmon (Rawas) cut in slices 2 cm
(¾ inch) thick

2 medium onions, finely sliced

2 tablespoons finely chopped fresh
coriander

3 green chillies, finely chopped

1 green chilli, slit

6 cloves garlic, finely chopped (¾ teaspoon)

¼ teaspoon cumin seeds, slightly pounded,
or cumin seed powder

2 dessertspoons flour

2¼ teaspoons salt

6 cherry tomatoes

2 cups water

1 tablespoon vinegar ⎫
1 tablespoon Worcestershire   Blend
Sauce   ⎬ together
½ tablespoon sugar   in a bowl
1 egg   ⎭

3 tablespoons vegetable oil

METHOD

1. In a pan, heat oil and fry onion till soft and yellow (not brown). Drain excess oil.

2. Add coriander, chopped green chillies, slit green chilli, garlic and cumin seeds. Blend
well and cook on low heat for 5 minutes.

3. Add flour and blend to a smooth paste, then add water gradually and mix well. Bring
mixture to the boil, add 1 teaspoon salt and simmer, covered, on low heat for 10
minutes.

4. Add slices of fish, tomatoes and 1¼ teaspoons salt and continue cooking till fish is
cooked.

5. Let fish cool then add mixture of vinegar, Worcestershire Sauce, sugar and egg. Tilt
pan to allow mixture to flow evenly over fish. Place pan again on heat and cook
5 minutes longer before serving.

❏ Serves 4

Previous page—Chicken Farcha (page 39),
Facing page—Luganno Sas (page 25)

6. Fish in Green Masala

Fillets of fish cooked in a green chutney masala paste.

INGREDIENTS

½ kg (18 oz) fillets of fish (Pomfret or other white fleshed fish)

½ coconut grated or 4 tablespoons desiccated coconut ⎫

6 large cloves garlic

1 heaped teaspoon cumin seeds ⎬ Grind to a paste

4 tablespoons roughly chopped fresh coriander

1 large or 2 small onions

3 green chillies ⎭

1 teaspoon lemon juice

1 large onion, finely sliced

1½ teaspoons salt

2 tablespoons vegetable oil

METHOD

1. In a wide shallow pan heat oil and fry sliced onion in it till pale yellow and soft.
2. Add masala paste and cook for 5 minutes. Add lemon juice.
3. Gradually add ½ cup water and continue cooking 10 minutes more.
4. Add fillets of fish and salt and blend well. Simmer, covered, till fish is cooked.

❑ Serves 4

7. Crispy-Brown Fried Fish

This dish is tastiest with slices of Pomfret or Rawas (Indian Salmon)
but slices of fresh Surmai (Seer) can also be crisply fried to a delicious flavour.

INGREDIENTS

1 Pomfret weighing about 400 g (14 oz) cut into 2 cm (¾ inch) thick slices or slices of Indian Salmon (Rawas)

1 teaspoon turmeric powder
½ teaspoon chilli powder
1 teaspoon salt
Vegetable oil for frying
} Mix together

METHOD

1. Coat each slice of fish with mixture of turmeric powder, chilli powder and salt and marinate for at least 1 hour.

2. Pour oil in a frying pan upto a depth of 1¼ cm (½ inch) and heat to medium hot.

3. Place pieces of fish in it and fry. When one side of each slice of fish is brown and crisp turn it over and allow other side to brown.

4. Serve, freshly fried, with slices of lemon and grilled slices of tomato.

❑ Serves 4

8. Stuffed Salmon

Attractive in appearance and simple to cook,
Stuffed Salmon is an easy dish to prepare
for formal or informal meals.

INGREDIENTS

1 Indian Salmon (Rawas) or Seer (Surmai) weighing about 700 g (about 1¾ lbs)

1½ teaspoons salt for fish

2 large onions, finely sliced

1 large tomato, finely chopped

1½ tablespoons finely chopped fresh coriander

2 green chillies, finely chopped

2½ teaspoons salt

4 tablespoons vegetable oil

METHOD

1. Clean fish and remove centre bone.
2. Rub 1½ teaspoons salt on inside surface of fish.
3. In a frying pan heat oil and fry onion in it till soft and pale gold, not brown. Remove excess oil.
4. To onion add chopped tomatoes, coriander, chillies and 1 teaspoon salt and blend well. Cook 10 minutes.
5. Remove from heat and place onion mixture along middle of fish.
6. Place fish in a baking tray and pour some of the excess oil of onion mixture over fish.
7. Bake in a moderate oven 30 to 40 minutes or till fish is cooked.
8. Remove fish to serving platter, garnish with tomato and onion slices and parsley and serve.

❏ Serves 6

9. Sas-ni-Machhi

Fish in Red Sauce

Fillets of fish baked in a spicy red sauce.

INGREDIENTS

½ kg (18 oz) fillets of Pomfret or other white fleshy fish

3 tablespoons vegetable oil

2 onions, finely sliced

2 tablespoons finely chopped fresh coriander .

½ kg (9 oz) tomatoes, chopped small

2 or 3 fresh green chillies, slit and seeded

3 dried red chillies ⎤ Grind
1 teaspoon cumin seeds ⎬ masala to a
6 cloves garlic (¾ teaspoon) ⎦ paste*

1 cup water

1½ to 2 teaspoons salt

1½ desertspoons flour ⎤
1½ dessertspoons Worcestershire Sauce ⎥ Combine in bowl
1½ dessertspoons vinegar ⎬ and blend well
1 dessertspoon sugar ⎥
3 eggs ⎦

METHOD

1. In 3 tablespoons oil fry onion till brown. Drain excess oil.

2. Add ground masala and stir to blend masala and onions well. Cook for 5 minutes over low heat adding a tablespoon of water if mixture tends to stick to bottom of pan.

3. Add coriander, tomatoes and green chillies and cook for 2 minutes.

4. Add 1 cup water and let mixture simmer, covered, for 15 minutes.

5. Add fish fillets and salt and simmer, covered, till fish is cooked.

6. Allow mixture to cool, then add mixture of flour, Worcestershire Sauce, vinegar, sugar and eggs. Blend well, but do not stir with a spoon as fish might break up. Tilt pan by hand in a circular movement, to let mixture flow evenly into sauce.

7. Pour into oven-proof dish and bake 30 to 40 minutes until sauce is stiff and nicely browned on top.

❏ Serves 4

   * Or you may use ¾ lightly packed teaspoon of Mangal's ready ground "Red Chilli, Jeera And Garlic Paste."

10. Spicy Fried Fish

*Slices of fish coated with a sweet
and spicy masala paste and
fried in a generous amount of oil.*

INGREDIENTS

1 large Pomfret weighing about 400 g (14oz)
cut into 6 slices, or slices of Indian
Salmon (Rawas)

4 dried Kashmiri red chillies

12 medium cloves garlic
(1¼ teaspoons)

1 heaped teaspoon cumin seeds

½ teaspoon turmeric powder

1 teaspoon jaggery (gur)

1 teaspoon tamarind

⎫
⎬ Grind
⎭ to a
paste

1¼ teaspoons salt

4 tablespoons vegetable oil

METHOD

1. Mix salt into masala paste.

2. Wash slices of fish and coat evenly all over with masala paste. Let stand 2 to 3 hours.

3. Heat oil in a frying pan and place slices of fish in it. When one side of the slice of fish is cooked, turn over and cook other side.

4. Serve as soon as fish is ready, spooning the extra hot oil over fish in serving dish.

❑ Serves 4

11. Patra-ni-Machhi

Fish in Banana Leaf

A traditional dish at wedding dinners.
Slices of fish coated with green chutney, wrapped in banana leaves and steamed.
(Foil can be used instead of the banana leaves)

INGREDIENTS

2 large Pomfrets weighing together 800 g (1¾ lbs)

2 teaspoons salt

Chutney

For the chutney grind to a paste, the following ingredients:

1 fresh coconut, grated, or 8 tablespoons desiccated coconut

1 cup roughly chopped fresh coriander

8 green chillies (4 of them deseeded if chutney is not desired chilli hot)

1 teaspoon cumin seeds

6 large cloves garlic (1 teaspoon)

2 teaspoons sugar

1 teaspoon salt

2 teaspoons lemon juice

Banana leaves or foil

METHOD

1. Remove heads of fish if desired and cut each fish into 6 slices.

2. Cut large enough portions of banana leaves or foil to wrap each slice of fish. Hold each piece of banana leaf over a flame a few seconds to soften leaf and centre rib. Grease one side of each portion of leaf or foil.

3. Using about 1 teaspoon salt per fish, rub salt into each slice of fish.

4. Coat each slice of fish with chutney.

5. Lay a slice of fish on the greased side of a piece of banana leaf or foil and roll it up. Tie with thread. Do the same with the other slices of fish and steam or bake for 30 minutes or till fish is cooked.

❑ Serves 6 to 8

12. Fried Fresh Bombay Duck

*This unusual fish is found off the west coast of India
during the monsoon season and
is a delicacy which is very popular.*

INGREDIENTS

12 medium-sized fresh Bombay Ducks

1 teaspoon turmeric powder

1 teaspoon chilli powder

1 teaspoon salt or to taste

¼ teaspoon pepper

4 dessertspoons rice flour or
   4 dessertspoons plain flour

6 tablespoons vegetable oil for frying

METHOD

1. Clean out stomach portion of each Bombay Duck. Also be sure to remove two small thorny protrusions on either side of the Bombay Duck, near the tail. Cut off the head.

2. Rub some flour over each Bombay Duck, then wash thoroughly.

3. Place Bombay Duck in a plate or flat lid of pan, cover with another lid and place a heavy weight on it. Let stand for ½ hour allowing excess water to drain out.

4. Mix together turmeric powder, chilli powder, salt and pepper and rub all over each Bombay Duck.

5. Heat some oil in a "tava" or iron griddle, or heavy-bottomed frying pan, to boiling point.

6. Roll each Bombay Duck lightly in rice flour or plain flour and fry till golden.

7. Serve at once with a generous squeeze of lemon juice on each.

❑ Serves 4 to 6

13. Fried Dried Bombay Duck

A liking for the unusual flavour and strong smell of dried
Bombay Duck is an acquired taste.
But it is worth acquiring for this delectable fish adds piquancy to many bland dishes.

INGREDIENTS

6 large dried Bombay Ducks

$1/3$ teaspoon turmeric powder

$1/3$ teaspoon chilli powder

¾ teaspoon salt or to taste

Vegetable oil for frying

METHOD

1. Cut off heads of Bombay Duck and any fin-like protrusions near the tail.

2. Cut each Bombay Duck into 4 pieces.

3. Mix together the turmeric powder, chilli powder and salt and rub evenly over pieces of Bombay Duck.

4. Let stand half to one hour.

5. Pour oil in a frying pan to a depth of 1 cm (½ inch) and heat. Fry pieces of Bombay Duck in it till crisp and brown.

6. Serve as an accompaniment to Masoor (p. 123) or any other "dal" (lentils).

14. Sooka Boomla Patio

Dried Bombay Duck Patio

Curried dry Bombay Duck usually eaten with Khichdee (Kedgeree).

INGREDIENTS

12 dried Bombay Duck

6 large cloves garlic

4 dried red Kashimiri chillies

2 teaspoons cumin seeds

1 onion, finely sliced

½ cup plus 1 tablespoon vinegar

2½ tablespoons grated jaggery

1 teaspoon salt

2 tablespoons vegetable oil

METHOD

1. Soak jaggery in ¼ cup vinegar.

2. Remove head and tail from each Bombay Duck and any fin-like protrusions near the tail. Cut each Bombay Duck into 4 pieces.

3. Grind to a paste garlic, red chillies and cumin seeds with 1 tablespoon vinegar.

4. In a pan, heat oil and fry onion till brown.

5. Add masala paste and cook 5 minutes.

6. Add pieces of Bombay Duck and mix well.

7. Add salt and ¼ cup vinegar and cook 3 minutes.

8. Add vinegar and jaggery mixture and 1 cup water, cover and cook on low heat 10 minutes or till Bombay Ducks are soft and cooked.

9. Serve with plain Khichdee or Vegetable Khichdee (p. 91).

❑ Serves 4

Chicken

It is traditional to serve chicken on "good" days in a Parsi home which, on festive occasions, is bustling with relatives and friends who expect and look forward to a hearty meal. Traditional dishes like "Khari Murghi-ma Sali" (Chicken with Potato Straws) and "Chicken Farcha" (Crumb-Fried Chicken) are always popular, but a change is equally welcome and appreciated.

It has been said that after a good meal one can forgive anybody, even one's own relatives, and the truth of it is proved in the happy, noisy camaraderie always obvious on such festive holidays.

15. Chicken Vindaloo

*Vindaloos are very popular and the recipe
given below can be varied by substituting mutton,
pork or fish for chicken.*

INGREDIENTS

1¼ kg (2½ lbs) chicken skinned
and cut into 8 pieces

2 large onions, finely sliced

4 to 8 dried red
Kashimiri chillies

8 cloves garlic
(1 teaspoon)

2½ cm (1 inch) piece
of fresh ginger root

1 teaspoon cumin seeds

} Grind to a
paste with
2 tablespoons
vinegar

4 tablespoons vinegar

5 cm (2 inches) piece cinnamon stick

2 to 4 green chillies, slit and seeded
(optional)

½ teaspoon sugar

1½ teaspoons salt

3 tablespoons vegetable oil

½ kg (9 oz) small potatoes, peeled

METHOD

1. Heat oil and fry onion in it till pale gold.

2. Add masala paste and cook 5 minutes.

3. Add pieces of chicken, 2 tablespoons vinegar, cinnamon stick, green chillies and salt
   and cook 10 minutes.

4. Add 1 cup hot water, bring to the boil then simmer, covered, till chicken is cooked
   or cook chicken in pressure cooker 20 minutes.

5. 15 minutes before chicken is ready, add potatoes and allow chicken and potatoes to
   cook together.

6. When chicken is cooked add sugar, taste and add more if desired.

❑ Serves 4

16. Chicken Mi-Vahlans

Chicken cooked in a creamy sauce,
then shredded and baked with raisins,
fried onions and potato squares.

INGREDIENTS

1¼ kg (2¼ lbs) chicken, skinned and cut
   into 8 pieces

5 large onions, finely sliced

6 cloves garlic (¾ teaspoon) ⎫

2½ cm (1 inch) piece of   ⎬ Grind
   fresh ginger root (¾ teaspoon)   to a

½ teaspoon cumin seeds   ⎭ paste

2 tablespoons butter

2 dessertspoons vegetable oil

2 tomatoes, roughly cut into 8 pieces each

¼ teaspoon pepper

3½ cm (1½ inches) cinnamon stick

2 whole dried red chillies

2½ to 3 teaspoons salt

1 dessertspoon flour

1¼ cups milk

½ cup cream

4 medium potatoes, peeled and cut into
   1cm (½ inch) squares

50 g (2 tablespoons) kismis
   (seedless raisins)

2 eggs

More oil for frying potatoes

METHOD

1. Heat butter and oil and fry 1 onion in it till pale gold.

2. Add paste of garlic, ginger and cumin seeds and cook 3 minutes.

3. Add pieces of chicken and fry chicken on high heat till nicely browned.

4. Add tomato, pepper, cinnamon stick, chillies and 1¼ tsp salt and mix well.

5. Add 1 cup water and bring to boil. Lower heat, cover and simmer till chicken is cooked.

6. Remove pieces of chicken from gravy and keep aside.

7. In a small bowl mix flour and 4 dessertspoons milk to a smooth paste and then add to gravy. Pour remaining milk into gravy and bring gravy to boil. Boil 3 minutes.

8. Strain gravy through a sieve and discard chillies and cinnamon stick.

9. Add cream to gravy. Heat gravy and simmer 3 minutes.

10. Shred chicken, discard bones and add chicken flesh to gravy.

11. In 6 tablespoons oil fry 4 onions till brown. Remove and keep aside.

12. Boil potato squares for 2 or 3 minutes in 2 cups water with 1½ teaspoons salt. Strain.

13. Pour oil in a frying pan to a depth of 1 cm (½ inch). Heat to boiling.

14. Add potato squares and fry till cooked and golden. Remove and keep aside.

15. In the same oil, fry kismis for 2 minutes. Remove and keep aside.

16. In a baking dish pour half chicken mixture. Over this sprinkle half the fried onions, potato squares and kismis.

17. Over this pour remaining chicken mixture and sprinkle other half of fried onions, potato squares and kismis.

18. Separate whites from yolks of eggs. Beat egg whites till stiff then blend in egg yolks.

19. Spread beaten eggs over chicken mixture and bake in moderate oven till eggs are set.

20. Serve at once.

❏ Serves 6

17. Chicken Farcha

*Pieces of chicken marinated in a gently-flavoured masala paste,
dipped in crumbs and beaten eggs and fried.*

INGREDIENTS

1 tender, medium (chicken) (1¼ kg (2½ lbs)) skinned and cut into 8 pieces

6 cloves garlic (¾ teaspoon)

2 cm (¾ inch) piece of fresh ginger root

4 tablespoons roughly chopped fresh coriander

2 to 4 green chillies

1 teaspoon cumin seeds

1 small onion, cut into 2 pieces

Grind to a paste

1 tablespoon Worcestershire Sauce

1 teaspoon salt

1 dessertspoon olive or salad oil

1 slightly heaped teaspoon flour

¾ cup dried breadcrumbs

2 eggs

Vegetable oil for frying

METHOD

1. Remove sections of bone from breast pieces of chicken.

2. With a sharp knife and with quick strong strokes cut into the flesh of each piece of chicken. The flesh should be slightly broken up but not cut right through.

3. Mix Worcestershire Sauce, salad oil, salt and flour into masala paste.

4. Coat each piece of chicken with the masala paste and allow chicken to marinate 8 to 10 hours. (If chicken is not very tender boil it before applying masala paste).

5. Pour oil in a deep frying pan upto a depth of 2½ cm (1 inch) and heat to medium hot.

6. While oil is heating, separate the eggs. Beat egg whites till frothy, then blend in egg yolks.

7. Coat each piece of chicken with breadcrumbs, dip in beaten eggs and fry on medium heat. Turn when one side is cooked and continue cooking till chicken is tender.

8. Serve with boiled potatoes and carrots cut into small squares and mixed with boiled peas, all smeared with melted butter.

❑ Serves 4

18. Chicken Mulligatawney

*Mulligatawney needs no introduction as the soup is famous.
This recipe for Chicken Mulligatawney, however, is a variation and is more like a curry.
It is enjoyed as a main course on its own or accompanied by rice.*

INGREDIENTS

1¼ (2½ lbs) chicken, skinned and cut into 8 pieces

2 medium onions, finely sliced

6 cloves garlic (¾ teaspoon)

2 cm (¾ inch) piece of fresh ginger root

3 dried red Kashimiri chillies

3 teaspoons coriander seeds

½ teaspoon cumin seeds

4 teaspoons poppy seeds (khus khus)

1 medium onion

4 cups meat or chicken stock or 4 cups water

6 curry leaves (curry patta)

2 large potatoes, cut into 6 to 8 pieces each

2½ teaspoons salt

6 tablespoons vegetable oil

1 fresh coconut, grated*

Juice of 1 lemon

METHOD

1. In a heavy-bottomed frying pan or on a "tava" slightly roast the coriander seeds, cumin seeds and poppy seeds. Then grind them to a masala paste together with garlic, ginger, chillies and 1 medium onion.

2. Add ¼ cup hot water to grated coconut and let stand 15 minutes. Then squeeze the coconut by hand to extract juice. Strain liquid and keep aside in a bowl.

3. Add ¼ cup more hot water to coconut and repeat process to extract juice again. Strain and keep aside in another bowl.

4. In a pan heat oil and fry finely sliced onion in it till golden. Drain excess oil.

5. Add masala paste and cook 10 minutes adding a little water to prevent it from sticking to bottom of pan.

  * If fresh coconut is not available, use 55 g (2 oz.) Cream of Coconut and ½ cup water or use 15 g coconut powder and ½ cup water.

6. Add pieces of chicken and brown nicely, then add 1½ cup soup stock or warm water, salt, curry patta and second bowl of coconut milk and simmer, covered, till chicken is tender and 1½ cups gravy remain.

7. 15 minutes before chicken is ready, add the potatoes. Remove potatoes when they are cooked.

8. Pour oil in a frying pan to a depth of 1 cm (½ inch) and fry potatoes in it till nice and brown. Return potatoes to pan with chicken.

9. Add first bowl of coconut milk and simmer 5 minutes.

10. Just before serving add lemon juice and heat.

11. If desired serve with 1 cup boiled rice or serve chicken on its own.

❑ Serves 4

19. Khari Murgi-ma Sali

Chicken with Potato Straws

Chicken in a typical brown gravy served with fine, crisp potato straws.

INGREDIENTS

1¼ kg (2½ lbs) chicken, skinned and cut into 8 pieces

2 medium onions, finely sliced

6 cloves garlic (¾ teaspoon) ⎫
2 cm (¾ inch) piece fresh ginger root ⎭ Grind to a paste

5 cm (2 inches) piece cinnamon stick

1¼ teaspoons salt

3 tablespoons vegetable oil

Potato straws from ½ kg potatoes (p. 67)

METHOD

1. Heat oil in a pan and fry onion in it till dark brown. Remove excess oil.

2. Add garlic-ginger paste and blend well. Cook 2 minutes and add a little water if paste sticks to bottom of pan.

3. Add pieces of chicken and brown nicely, then add cinnamon stick, 1 cup warm water and salt and simmer, covered, till chicken is cooked.

4. To serve, place pieces of chicken and gravy in serving dish and sprinkle potato straws over them.

❑ Serves 4

20. Chicken with Cashewnuts

Nuts are often used in Parsi recipes to give both body
and flavour to a gravy.
The recipe below is enriched with cashewnuts.

INGREDIENTS

1¼ kg (2½ lbs) chicken, skinned
and cut into 8 pieces

10 cloves garlic (1¼ teaspoons) ⎫
                     ⎬ Grind to a paste
2 cm (¾ inch) piece of fresh ⎭
ginger root

1 medium onion, finely sliced

4 dried Kashimiri red chillies ⎫
                     ⎬ Grind to a paste
½ teaspoon cumin seeds ⎭

15 to 20 cashewnuts, ground to a paste

3 tablespoons tomato ketchup

½ teaspoon sugar

1½ teaspoons salt

2 tablespoons vegetable oil

METHOD

1. Rub garlic-ginger paste over pieces of chicken and allow to marinate 1 hour.

2. Heat oil in a pan and fry onion in it till golden.

3. Add chilli paste and cook 5 minutes, adding a little water if paste sticks to bottom of pan.

4. Add chicken and cook 5 minutes.

5. Add 1 cup warm water and salt and let simmer 15 minutes.

6. When chicken is half cooked, add cashewnut paste and continue simmering chicken, covered, till tender.

7. Add tomato ketchup and sugar and cook 5 minutes more before serving. Serve with potato chips.

❑ Serves 4

21. Chicken in Milk

Chicken has a delicious and subtle flavour when cooked with milk.

INGREDIENTS

1¼ kg (2½ lbs) chicken, skinned
and cut into 8 pieces

2 medium onions, finely sliced

6 cloves garlic (¾ teaspoon) ⎫
2 cm (¾ inch) piece of fresh ⎬ Grind to
ginger root ⎭ a paste

5 cm (2 inches) piece
cinnamon stick

1 dried red chilli

Salt as needed

1 cup milk

1 teaspoon sugar

4 tablespoons vegetable oil

3 potatoes

1 tablespoon kismis (seedless raisins)

METHOD

1. Heat oil and fry onion till golden. Remove excess oil.

2. Add garlic-ginger paste and blend well. Cook 5 minutes, adding a little water if paste sticks to bottom of pan.

3. Add chicken, blend well and allow chicken to brown nicely on all sides (about 10 minutes).

4. Add cinnamon stick, whole red chilli and 1¼ tsp salt. Mix well.

5. Add ¾ cup warm water, bring to the boil and simmer, covered, till chicken is tender and ½ cup gravy remains. Add more water if necessary.

6. Add milk and sugar and allow to boil, uncovered, for 10 to 15 minutes till some of the milk has dried away and the gravy is thick.

7. Peel potatoes and cut them into tiny squares. Pour oil in frying pan to a depth of 1 cm (½ inch). Heat to medium hot and fry potatoes in it till crisp and golden. Remove and set aside. Sprinkle with salt.

8. Fry kismis for 1 minute in same oil and remove.

9. Place chicken with gravy in serving dish and sprinkle with potatoes and kismis.

❑ Serves 4

MEAT

Meat, mostly in the form of mutton, is included daily in a Parsi menu. The day's fare is not complete without it and the ways of cooking and presenting meat are varied and many.

Perhaps the most typical and popular meat dish is "Kharoo Gosh"— meat cooked with onion, garlic and ginger, which gives a delicate and delicious flavour to the brown gravy. This basic recipe is used in innumerable dishes to which different vegetables are added. However, there are several other typical ways of cooking meat — in the form of mince, cutlets and chops and with herbs and gravies of different flavours, which add variety, colour and interest to the dishes.

22. Boti-Soti

Marinated pieces of meat speared onto fine wooden skewers with small potatoes and onions, coated with crumbs and egg and fried.

INGREDIENTS

½ kg (18 oz.) mutton cut into
  2 cm (¾ inch) cubes

6 cloves garlic (¾ teaspoon) ⎫

2 cm (¾ inch) piece of   ⎬ Grind to
  fresh ginger root   a paste

2 dried red chillies ⎭

1½ tablespoons Worcestershire Sauce

¾ tablespoon salad oil

½ teaspoon pepper

2½ teaspoons salt

12 small potatoes, peeled

12 button onions, peeled

2 eggs

½ cup dried breadcrumbs

Vegetable oil for frying

6 fine wooden skewers (satay sticks)
  each 8 inches long, to use as skewers

METHOD

1. Mix together chilli paste, Worcestershire Sauce, salad oil, pepper and 1 teaspoon salt. Marinate meat in mixture at least 2 hours.

2. In a pan heat 2 tablespoons oil and add meat. Cook on low heat, uncovered, till all the water from the meat has dried. Add 2 cups water and cook meat till done. Drain any excess liquid.

3. Take pan off heat and allow meat to cool.

4. Boil potatoes for 2 minutes in water to which 1½ teaspoons salt has been added. Drain.

5. Pierce 1 or 2 pieces of meat with a skewer, then a potato and an onion. Repeat once more and end with a piece of meat. Complete all the lengths of skewers similarly.

6. In a frying pan, pour oil to a depth of 2 cm (¾ inch) and heat. Place sticks in oil and fry till meat, potatoes and onions are nicely browned and the meat is fork tender.

7. Add more oil to frying pan to a depth of 2 cm (¾ inch) and heat.

8. Beat eggs till light and frothy.

9. Roll the skewers with meat, potatoes and onions in breadcrumbs, dip in beaten eggs and fry till golden brown.

10. Serve on their own or on a bed of Tomato Rice (p. 90).

❏ Makes 6

23. Crumb-Fried Lamb Chops

*Tender lamb chops are marinated in a gently spiced
green chilli paste, coated with crumbs and egg and fried.*

INGREDIENTS

6 large lamb chops from rib section

6 cloves garlic (¾ teaspoon)

2 cm (¾ inch) piece of fresh ginger root

1 small onion, roughly chopped

2 or 3 green chillies, (seeded if desired)

1 teaspoon cumin seeds

2 tablespoons chopped fresh coriander

} Grind to a paste

1 tablespoon salad oil

1 tablespoon Worcestershire Sauce

1 teaspoon salt

2 eggs

½ cup dried breadcrumbs

Vegetable oil for frying

METHOD

1. Flatten and score each chop by beating with the sharp edge of a knife being careful not to cut right through the meat.

2. Mix salt into the masala paste and coat each chop with the paste. Place chops in a plate.

3. Mix salad oil and Worcestershire Sauce in a small bowl and pour half the mixture over the chops. Turn the chops over and pour the remaining mixture over them.

4. Allow chops to marinate 1 or 2 hours.

5. Spread breadcrumbs in a plate and press each chop into them till all chops are well coated on both sides.

6. In a frying pan pour oil to a depth of 1 cm (½ inch) and heat to medium hot.

7. While oil is heating, break eggs into a soup plate and beat with a fork till they are light and frothy.

8. Dip each chop in beaten egg and place gently in frying pan. Cook till meat is tender.

9. Serve with mashed potato and boiled peas or Fried Bananas (p. 112).

24. Meat Cutlets in Tomato Gravy

A very traditional, and one of the most popular dishes,
in which the cutlets are cooked,
then soaked and heated in a special tomato gravy.

INGREDIENTS

For Cutlets

½ kg (18 oz.) mutton, minced

1 medium onion, minced with meat or chopped very fine

6 cloves garlic (¾ teaspoon) ⎱ Grind to
2½ cm (1 inch) piece of ⎰ a paste
fresh ginger root ⎰ (1 teaspoon)

¾ teaspoon turmeric powder

2 to 4 green chillies, finely chopped

2 tablespoons finely chopped fresh coriander

3 slices bread (100 g or 4 oz)

2 dessertspoons Worcestershire Sauce

8 leaves fresh mint, chopped

1 teaspoon salt

2 eggs

¾ cup dried breadcrumbs

Vegetable oil for frying

For Tomato Gravy

½ kg (18 oz) ripe, red tomatoes

3½ cm (1½ inches) piece cinnamon stick

1 green chilli

8 to 10 leaves fresh mint

2 cloves

1 onion, finely sliced

½ teaspoon cumin seeds ⎱ Grind to
4 cloves garlic ⎰ a paste
1 dried red chilli ⎰

1 dessertspoon vinegar

1 dessertspoon sugar or to taste

1 teaspoon salt

2 tablespoons vegetable oil

METHOD

Cutlets

1. Soak bread in water for 10 minutes. Remove and squeeze dry. Add to minced meat.

2. Add all other ingredients except eggs, breadcrumbs and oil to minced meat. Mix well, cover and leave to marinate at least 1 hour.

3. Divide minced meat mixture into 12 equal portions and shape into cutlets.

4. Spread breadcrumbs in a plate or other flat surface and press each cutlet in it till all sides are coated.

5. Separate eggs, and beat egg whites till frothy. Add yolks and blend well.

6. In a frying pan, pour oil to a depth of 1 cm (½ inch) and heat to medium hot.

7. Dip each cutlet in beaten eggs and fry till golden brown, on both sides, turing once.

Tomato Gravy

1. Cut tomatoes in half and cook in 1 tablespoon water with cinnamon stick, whole green chilli, mint and cloves till tomatoes are very soft.

2. Remove cinnamon stick, chilli and cloves and mash tomatoes through a sieve to get tomato juice. Discard pulp.

3. In the oil fry onion till golden brown. Remove excess oil.

4. Add ground masala paste and cook 5 minutes adding 1 dessertspoon water at a time if masala sticks to bottom of pan.

5. Add tomato juice, vinegar, sugar and salt and cook till sauce has thickened.

6. Add cutlets to tomato gravy and cook on low heat till cutlets have absorbed as much gravy as possible. Turn cutlets once.

7. Place cutlets with gravy in large platter and serve with boiled green peas and potato chips or mashed potato.

❏ Serves 6

25. Mutton Baffat

A curried mutton stew.

INGREDIENTS

350 g (¾ lb) mutton cut into
2½ cm (1 inch) cubes

½ fresh coconut, grated, or
4 tablespoons desiccated
coconut

8 cloves garlic (1 teaspoon)

2½ cm (1 inch) piece
of fresh ginger root

4 to 6 dried red Kashimiri
chillies

1 teaspoon cumin seeds

¾ teaspoon turmeric powder

1 dessertspoon sesame
seeds (til)

2 teaspoons peanuts

2 teaspoons shelled gram
(chickpea)

1 small onion, cut into
2 pieces

} Grind to
a paste

½ cup tamarind juice from 1 heaped
tablespoon tamarind pulp (p. 17) or
1½ tablespoons vinegar

1½ tablespoons grated jaggery

6 drumsticks

4 medium potatoes, peeled and each cut
into 4 pieces

2 carrots, scraped and cut into 2½ cm
(1 inch) pieces

8 button onions, peeled

Salt to taste

3 tablespoons vegetable oil

METHOD

1. Boil meat in 4 cups water with ¾ teaspoon salt, or pressure cook in 2 cups water.

2. Remove 1 strand of "thread" down the length of 1 drumstick. Cut the drumstick into 4 pieces then tie pieces in a "bundle" with the "thread." Prepare remaining drumsticks in the same way. (See picture below)

3. Boil drumsticks adding 2 teaspoons salt, with potatoes, carrots and onions till vegetables are half cooked. Drain.

4. In a deep pan heat oil to medium hot then add masala paste and cook, stirring, 10 minutes. Add 2 cups meat stock and cook 5 minutes. Add meat, potatoes, carrots and onions and cook, covered, on low heat, till potatoes and carrots are tender. Add drumsticks.

5. Add tamarind juice or vinegar and jaggery. Simmer till jaggery has melted then remove from heat.

6. Serve piping hot.

❑ Serves 4

26. Bharuchi Kid

A very special Parsi way of cooking meat of young lamb.

INGREDIENTS

¾ kg (1¾ lbs) meat of young lamb cut into large 4 cm (1½ inch) square pieces

⅓ cup milk of ¼ fresh grated coconut, (p. 16)*

1½ large onions, finely sliced

3 cloves garlic ⎤

1 cm (½ inch) piece of fresh ginger root ⎬ Grind to a paste

2 tablespoons cashewnuts ⎦

2½ cm (1 inch) stick cinnamon

2 dried red chillies

1 cardamom, peeled

½ kg (6 medium) potatoes peeled and cut in half lengthwise

1¼ cups milk

3 teaspoons salt

3 tablespoons vegetable oil

METHOD

1. In a pan, heat oil and fry onion in it till golden. Remove excess oil.

2. Add garlic-ginger paste and cook 5 minutes, adding a little water if paste tends to stick to bottom of pan.

3. Add pieces of meat, cinnamon stick, whole red chillies and cardamom and cook till meat is nicely browned (about 15 minutes).

4. Add 2 cups warm water, potatoes and salt and cook, covered, on low heat till meat is half cooked and water almost evaporated.

5. Remove pan from heat and allow to cool a while.

6. Remove potatoes from pan and keep aside.

7. To the meat, add coconut milk and fresh milk and return to heat. Cook, covered, till meat is tender.

8. In a frying pan pour oil to a depth of 1 cm (½ inch). Heat, then fry potatoes in it till golden and crisp.

9. Return potatoes to meat, heat all together and serve in a large platter.

❑ Serves 6

* Or use 25g (about I oz) Cream of Coconut and ⅓ cup water, or use coconut powder (p. 19).

27. Khatoo Mithoo Gosh

Sweet and Sour Meat

Meat cooked in a sweet and sour gravy.

INGREDIENTS

½ kg (18 oz) mutton, cut in 2 cm (¾ inch) cubes

2 large onions, finely sliced

6 cloves garlic (¾ teaspoon) ⎫

2 cm (¾ inch) piece of fresh ginger root

1 teaspoon cumin seeds

3 to 4 dried red Kashimiri chillies ⎭

Grind to a paste*

½ kg (18 oz) small potatoes

¾ cup shelled peas

1 tablespoon vinegar

1 tablespoon Worcestershire Sauce

1 tablespoon sugar

2½ teaspoons salt

4 tablespoons vegetable oil

METHOD

1. Boil potatoes in water for 2 minutes, peel and keep aside.

2. Heat oil in a deep pan and fry onion in it till dark brown. Drain excess oil.

3. Add the masala paste, blend well and cook for 5 minutes, adding 1 dessertspoon water at a time if the masala sticks to bottom of pan.

4. Add meat, blend well with masala and allow to cook 15 minutes, or till the water from the meat has evaporated.

5. Add 1 cup water and 1 teaspoon salt and let simmer. After 10 minutes, add 3 more cups water, cover and continue to simmer or pressure cook the meat with 1 cup water.

6. When meat is nearly cooked, add the potatoes and 1 teaspoon salt and continue cooking till meat and potatoes are done.

7. Add vinegar, Worcestershire Sauce and sugar and cook 5 minutes.

8. Boil peas adding ½ teaspoon salt, drain and sprinkle over meat mixture in serving dish.

❑ Serves 4

* Or you may use 1 lightly packed teaspoon of Mangal's "Red Chilli, Jeera And Garlic Paste."

53

28. Turela Bhinda-ma Kharoo Gosh

Meat with Fried Okra

*Meat in a brown gravy, flavoured with garlic and ginger
and served with fried bhindi (okra).*

INGREDIENTS

½ kg (18 oz) mutton cut into
2 cm (¾ inch) cubes

1 large onion, finely sliced

3 tablespoons vegetable oil

6 cloves garlic (¾ teaspoon) ⎤ Grind to

2 cm (¾ inch) piece of fresh ⎬ a paste
ginger root ⎦ (1 teaspoon)

8 cm (3 inches) cinnamon stick

½ kg (18 oz) bhindi (okra)

1¾ teaspoons salt

Vegetable oil for frying

METHOD

1. Heat 3 tablespoons oil in a pan and fry onion in it till brown. Drain excess oil.

2. Add garlic-ginger paste and blend well. Cook 5 minutes adding a little water if paste sticks to bottom of pan.

3. Add meat and brown nicely about 15 minutes till all the water has dried.

4. Add 1 cup water, cinnamon stick and 1 teaspoon salt and simmer, covered, 10 minutes.

5. Gradually add 3 more cups warm water and continue simmering, covered, till meat is cooked and I cup gravy remains. Or pressure cook meat with 1 cup water.

6. Cut bhindi into 2½ cm (1 inch) pieces and sprinkle ¾ teaspoon salt over them. Keep 15 to 20 minutes. Pour oil into a frying pan to a depth of 1½ cm (½ inch) and heat.

7. Gently fry the bhindi in it and remove.

8. Add fried bhindi to meat, heat all together for 10 minutes before serving.

❏ Serves 4

29. Cauliflower-ma Gosh

Meat and Cauliflower

Meat in brown gravy, cooked with cauliflower and finished with the delicate flavour of coconut milk.

INGREDIENTS

½ kg (18 oz) mutton cut into small cubes

2 medium heads cauliflower

2 cups milk of 1 fresh grated coconut*
(p. 16)

2 large onions, finely sliced

2 large onions, finely chopped

6 cloves garlic (¾ teaspoon) ⎤ Grind to a
2 cm (¾ inch) piece of   ⎬ paste
  fresh ginger root   ⎦ (1 teaspoon)

5 cm (2 inches) piece cinnamon stick

3 to 4 whole dried red chillies

2½ teaspoons salt

4 tablespoons vegetable oil

METHOD

1. Break up cauliflower into florets.

2. Heat oil and fry 2 finely sliced onions till brown. Drain excess oil.

3. Add garlic and ginger paste and cook 5 minutes.

4. Add meat and brown nicely for 10 minutes.

5. Add cinnamon stick, red chilli, 3 cups warm water and 1 teaspoon salt. Cover and cook on low heat till meat is cooked and ¼ cup gravy remains.

6. Add coconut milk, cauliflower, finely chopped onion and 1½ teaspoons salt. Blend well, then cover and cook on low heat till meat and cauliflower are well cooked and ¾ cup thick gravy remains.

❑ Serves 6

* Or use 110 g (4 oz) Cream of Coconut plus 2 cups water, or coconut powder (p. 19)

30. Chops in Green Masala

Lamb chops fried, then cooked in spicy green masala.

INGREDIENTS

½ kg (18 oz) lamb chops from rib section

6 cloves garlic (¾ teaspoon)

2 cm (¾ inch) piece of fresh ginger root

1 dessertspoon poppy seeds (khus khus)

2½ cm (1 inch) stick cinnamon or
½ teaspoon cinnamon powder

3 green chillies

3 cloves

4 tablespoons semi-heaped, roughly
chopped fresh coriander

2 medium onions

½ teaspoon turmeric powder

1½ teaspoons salt

Vegetable oil as required

METHOD

1. Flatten the meat of the chops by beating gently in a quick motion with the sharp edge of a knife.

2. Grind the rest of the ingredients together, except salt and oil.

3. In a frying pan, heat 3 tablespoons oil and fry chops in it till nicely browned (about 5 minutes on each side).

4. In a deep pan, heat 1½ tablespoons oil and cook masala paste in it for 10 minutes, stirring frequently so that it does not stick to bottom of pan.

5. Add fried chops to masala paste and blend well.

6. Add salt and a minimum amount of water, from ½ cup to ¾ cup, and let simmer, covered, till chops are tender.

7. Serve with small potatoes, boiled, peeled and brushed with melted butter.

❑ Serves 3 to 4

*Facing page—Chops in Green Masala (page 56),
Overleaf—Bharuchi Kid (page 52)*

31. Papeta-ma Gosh

Meat and Potato Stew

*One of the best known Parsi dishes in which
meat is cooked with potatoes and peas.*

INGREDIENTS

¼ kg (9 oz) mutton cut into
   2 cm (¾ inch) cubes

1 onion, finely sliced

¼ kg (9 oz) potatoes (3 medium)

¼ cup shelled peas

6 cloves garlic (¾ teaspoon) ⎤
2 cm (¾ inch) piece of   ⎥ Grind to
   fresh ginger root   ⎥ a paste
1 medium onion   ⎥
¼ teaspoon cumin seeds   ⎦

2 green chillies, slit

5 cm (2 inches) piece cinnamon stick

2 cloves   ⎤
2 black peppercorns   ⎥ Powdered
   Powdered   ⎥
1 cardamom, peeled   ⎦

2 teaspoons salt

2 tablespoons vegetable oil

Extra oil for frying potatoes

METHOD

1. Peel potatoes and cut each potato into 4 pieces.
2. Heat 2 tablespoons oil and fry sliced onion in it till brown. Drain excess oil.
3. Add the paste of garlic, ginger, onion and cumin seeds and blend well. Cook 5 minutes.
4. Add meat and brown nicely and cook till water from meat has dried up.
5. Add potatoes, chillies, cinnamon stick, 1 cup water and 1½ teaspoons salt. Bring to the boil, then simmer, covered 20 minutes.
6. Add 3 more cups warm water and continue simmering.
7. When potatoes are cooked, remove them and keep aside.
8. Continue cooking meat till it is tender and 1½ cups gravy remains. Or pressure cook meat till almost done. Then open cooker, add potatoes. Pressure cook again, till meat and potatoes are cooked.
9. Boil peas adding ½ teaspoon salt. Drain.
10. In a frying pan, heat oil to a depth of 1 cm (½ inch) and fry pieces of potato in it till they are nice and brown.
11. Return them to meat mixture and add the powdered spices and peas.
12. Heat everything together for 5 minutes and serve.

❏ Serves 4

Previous page—Boti-Soti (page 46), Facing page—Khari Murgi-ma-Sali (page 42)

32. Meat Sakarkand

Meat with Sweet Potato

Meat in brown gravy served with fried slices of sweet potato in sugar syrup.

INGREDIENTS

½ kg (18 oz) mutton cut into
  2 cm (¾ inch) cubes

2 onions, finely sliced

6 cloves garlic (¾ teaspoon) ⎫ Grind to
2 cm (¾ pinch) piece of   ⎬ a paste
  fresh ginger root   ⎭ (1 teaspoon)

10 cm (4 inches) piece
  cinnamon stick
  (broken into 2 or 3 pieces)

1½ teaspoons salt

1 kg (2¼ lb) sweet potato

300 g (1⅓ cups) sugar

2 cardamoms, peeled and crushed
  (¼ teaspoon)

¼ teaspoon nutmeg powder

Vegetable oil as needed

METHOD

1. Heat 4 tablespoons oil in a pan and fry onion in it till brown. Drain excess oil.

2. To the onion add garlic and ginger paste and blend well. Cook 3 minutes adding 1 tablespoon water if mixture sticks to bottom of pan.

3. Add meat, blend well and cook till water from meat has dried up.

4. Add 3½ cups water, cinnamon stick and salt, bring to the boil, then lower heat and cook, covered, till meat is cooked and tender. Or Pressure cook meat with 1 cup water.

5. Boil sweet potatoes, cool slightly, then peel and slice into 1 cm (½ inch) thick rounds.

6. In a deep frying pan pour oil to a depth of 2½ cm (1 inch) and heat. Fry slices of sweet potato in it till golden brown on both sides. Remove and keep aside.

7. For the Sugar Syrup, put sugar with 1 cup water in a pan and cook to make thin sugar syrup.

8. To test, put a drop of syrup in a plate and let cool slightly. Take it up on a finger then

press between thumb and finger. Separate thumb and finger gently and see that there is one "strand" of the syrup between them.

9. Add slices of sweet potato to syrup and cook on low heat till sweet potato has absorbed enough syrup to become soft. Sprinkle cardamom and nutmeg powder.

10. To serve, place meat in centre of platter surrounded by sweet potato or serve in separate dishes.

❏ Serves 4

33. Meat with Apricots

Tiny pieces of mutton cooked in a traditional brown gravy and sweetened with apricots in sugar syrup.

INGREDIENTS

½ kg (18 oz) mutton, cut into
1 cm (½ inch) cubes

2 medium onions, finely sliced

1 onion, finely chopped

6 cloves garlic (¾ teaspoon) ⎤ Grind to
2 cm (¾ inch) piece of ⎬ a paste
fresh ginger root ⎦ (1 teaspoon)

5 cm (2 inches) piece cinnamon stick

1¼ teaspoons salt

4 tablespoons vegetable oil

200 g (8 oz) dried apricots soaked in
1 cup water at least for 4 hours

1 teaspoon sugar

METHOD

1. Fry finely sliced onion in 4 tablespoons oil till golden brown. Drain excess oil, leaving only 1 tablespoon in pan.

2. Add garlic and ginger paste and cook 5 minutes.

3. Add meat and chopped onion and cook till meat water has evaporated.

4. Add cinnamon stick, salt and ½ cup warm water and simmer, covered, 15 minutes.

5. Add 2½ cups water and continue simmering, covered, till meat is tender and ½ cup gravy remains. Or pressure cook meat in 1 cup water till meat is tender.

6. Put 1 teaspoon sugar in a small pan. Place pan on medium heat and allow sugar to brown.

7. When sugar is a very dark brown colour, add soaked apricots together with the water in which they were soaked.

8. Bring to the boil, lower heat, cover and cook for 10 or 15 minutes till apricots are soft.

9. Carefully remove seeds from apricots, then add apricots, together with their syrup, to the meat.

10. Heat meat mixture and serve, sprinkled with potato straws (p. 67) made from ¼ kg (9 oz) potatoes.

❑ Serves 4

34. Papdi-ma-Kavab

*A very typical Parsi dish made with a flat beanlike vegetable called
"papdi" in Gujarati and "sem" in Punjabi.
Minced meat kavabs are cooked with it for blended flavours.*

INGREDIENTS

For Kavabs

¼ kg (9 oz) minced mutton

1 small onion, minced with the meat, or finely chopped

1½ slices bread (50g or 2 oz)

4 cloves garlic (½ teaspoon) ⎫ Grind to
1 cm (½ inch) piece of   ⎬ a paste
fresh ginger root   ⎭ (¾ teaspoon)

½ teaspoon turmeric powder

1 or 2 green chillies, finely chopped

2 teaspoons finely chopped fresh mint leaves

¼ teaspoon chilli powder

¼ teaspoon Dhansak masala

1½ tablespoons lightly packed, finely chopped, fresh coriander

1 egg

¾ teaspoon salt

2 tablespoons dried breadcrumbs

Vegetable oil for frying

For Papdi

350 g (about ¾ lb) small papdi (sem)

1 cm (½ inch) piece of fresh ⎫
ginger root   ⎪
6 cloves garlic (¾ teaspoon) ⎬ Grind to
                               ⎪ a paste
2 or 3 green chillies   ⎪
2 cloves   ⎭

1 onion, finely sliced

½ teaspoon carom seeds (ajwain)

1 teaspoon Dhansak masala

½ teaspoon turmeric powder

½ pod green garlic (optional) finely chopped

½ pod garlic

2 tablespoons finely chopped fresh coriander

3 spring onions, finely chopped

1¼ teaspoons salt

Vegetable oil

METHOD

Kavabs

1. Soak slices of bread in water for 10 minutes. Remove from water and squeeze dry.

2. Mix all ingredients, except dried breadcrumbs and oil, with the soaked bread and blend well.

3. Divide mixture into small balls about 2 cm (¾ inch) in diameter.

4. Roll each ball in the dried breadcrumbs till lightly coated all over.

5. Pour enough oil in a "kadai" (wok-shaped pan) or skillet, for deep-frying. Heat to medium hot and gently fry the meat balls in it.

6. Remove when nicely browned, and set aside.

Papdi

1. Remove threads from along the sides of each papdi as in french beans. If the papdi is small, keep whole. If it is longer than 4 cm (1½ inches), then cut in half.

2. Heat 2 tablespoons oil and fry sliced onion in it till brown.

3. To the fried onion, add masala paste, carom seeds, Dhansak masala and turmeric powder and cook 5 minutes till the mixture exudes an aroma.

4. Add green garlic, coriander, spring onion, ½ pod of garlic and salt. Cook for 5 minutes then add papdi and cook 5 minutes more. Add 1 cup water and cover and cook till papdi is tender and ¾ cup gravy remains.

5. Now add kavabs to papdi and continue cooking for 5 minutes. Turn the kavabs gently so as not to break them and continue cooking 5 minutes longer till flavours are well blended.

❏ Serves 4

35. Brain Cutlets

An attractive and tasty way of serving brain.

INGREDIENTS

4 sheep's brains

1 large onion, finely chopped

2 green chillies, finely chopped

½ teaspoon turmeric powder

1 tablespoon chopped fresh coriander

¾ teaspoon salt

½ cup dried breadcrumbs

1 egg

Vegetable oil for frying

METHOD

1. Soak brains in cold water for 10 or 15 minutes. Remove from water and clean by removing fine outer skin and blood vessels and the 2 white "beads" at the bottom of each brain.

2. Cut each brain into 4 to 6 pieces.

3. Place brain in a pan with the onion, green chilli, turmeric powder, coriander and salt and cook without water a few minutes, stirring, till brain is cooked and mashed by the stirring. Cool.

4. Add 1 tablespoon breadcrumbs to brain mixture. Shape mixture into 8 cutlets (If mixture sticks to the hand, wet hands before handling mixture).

5. Coat each cutlet with breadcrumbs. Break the egg into a soup plate and beat with a fork till light and frothy.

6. Pour oil in a frying pan to a depth of 1 cm (½ inch) and heat to medium hot.

7. Dip each cutlet in beaten egg and fry till golden on both sides. Serve with mashed potato or with Sweet Carrots (p. 115)

❑ Serves 4

36. Khatoo Mithoo Bhejoo

Sweet and Sour Brain

Brain cooked with tomato in a sweet and sour gravy.

INGREDIENTS

4 sheep's brains

4 large onions, finely sliced

6 cloves garlic (¾ teaspoon) ⎫
2 cm (¾ inch) piece of   ⎬ Grind to a paste (1 teaspoon)
fresh ginger root   ⎭

4 green chillies, finely chopped

1 tablespoon finely chopped fresh coriander

½ teaspoon turmeric powder

½ teaspoon chilli powder

2 large tomatoes, roughly chopped

2 dessertspoons vinegar

1 dessertspoon Worcestershire Sauce

1½ dessertspoons sugar

2 teaspoons salt or to taste

6 tablespoons vegetable oil

METHOD

1. Clean brains by soaking in cold water for 10 to 15 minutes, then carefully remove the outer skin and blood vessels. Also remove 2 white "beads" at the base of the brain, if not already removed by the butcher.

2. Cut each brain into 4 to 6 pieces.

3. In a pan heat oil and fry onion in it till soft and pale gold but not brown. Drain excess oil.

4. Add garlic-ginger paste, green chillies, coriander, turmeric powder and chilli powder and blend well for 2 minutes.

5. Add tomatoes and cook a few minutes till tomatoes are soft.

6. Add brain and salt, blend well gently and cook, a few minutes, covered, till brain is cooked.

7. Add vinegar, Worcestershire Sauce and sugar and simmer, covered, 5 minutes before serving.

8. If desired, sprinkle fried potato squares of 2 potatoes over brain to serve.

❑ Serves 4

37. Kharoo Bhejoo

Brain in Brown Gravy

Brain in brown gravy flavoured with garlic, ginger and fresh coriander.

INGREDIENTS

4 sheep's brains

$\frac{1}{3}$ teaspoon turmeric powder

2 large onions, finely sliced

3 cloves garlic ($\frac{1}{3}$ teaspoon)

1 cm ($\frac{1}{2}$ inch) piece or fresh ginger root

} Grind to a paste ($\frac{1}{2}$ teaspoon)

1 tablespoon finely chopped fresh coriander (optional)

1 green chilli, slit and seeded (optional)

1½ teaspoons salt

3 tablespoons vegetable oil

METHOD

1. Clean brains by soaking in cold water for 10 to 15 minutes, then carefully remove thin outer skin and blood vessels. Also remove 2 white "beads" at the base of the brain if not already removed by the butcher.

2. Boil brains in 2 cups water adding ¾ teaspoon salt and turmeric powder. When cooked, cool, then cut each brain into 6 pieces.

3. In a pan heat oil to medium hot and fry onion in it till light brown.

4. Add garlic and ginger paste and cook 5 minutes.

5. Add brain, ¾ teaspoon salt and ¾ cup water. Bring to the boil then simmer, uncovered, 10 minutes.

6. Add coriander and chilli and cook 5 minutes more then remove from heat and serve. Sprinkle fried potato squares over brain before serving if desired.

❑ Serves 4

38. Tamota-ma Gosh

Meat in Tomato

Meat cooked in tomato pulp with spices.

INGREDIENTS

350 g (13 oz) mutton cut into
  1½ cm (¾ inch) cubes

1 kg (2¼ lbs) ripe red tomatoes

2 large onions, finely sliced

4 cloves garlic
  (½ teaspoon)

1 cm (½ inch) piece of
  fresh ginger root

} Grind to
  a paste
  (¾ teaspoon)

½ teaspoon chilli powder

½ teaspoon turmeric powder

2 tablespoons finely chopped fresh
  coriander

5 cm (2 inches) piece cinnamon stick

4 teaspoons sugar

1¾ teaspoons salt

4 tablespoons vegetable oil

METHOD

1. Place tomatoes in very hot water a few minutes. Drain and remove skin from tomatoes. Chop them roughly and keep aside.

2. In a pan heat oil and fry onion in it till golden. Drain excess oil.

3. Add garlic-ginger paste, turmeric powder, chilli powder, coriander and cinnamon stick and cook 5 minutes.

4. Add meat and blend well. Cook till water from meat has dried, then add chopped tomato and salt. Bring mixture to the boil then simmer, covered, till meat is cooked and tender.

5. Add sugar and cook 5 minutes more, then remove from heat.

❏ Serves 4

39. Kheema-Sali

Mince with Potato Straws

*Sweet and sour minced meat served
with potato straws.*

INGREDIENTS

½ kg (18 oz) minced mutton

2 onions, finely sliced

6 cloves garlic (¾ teaspoon) ⎫

2 cm (¾ inch) piece of
   fresh ginger root   ⎬ Grind to a paste

4 dried red Kashimiri chillies

2 teaspoons cumin seeds ⎭

½ teaspoon turmeric powder

1 medium tomato, roughly chopped

1 teaspoon salt

1 tablespoon vinegar

1 tablespoon Worcestershire Sauce

1 tablespoon sugar

4 tablespoons vegetable oil

METHOD

1. In a pan heat oil, then fry onion in it till brown. Drain excess oil.

2. Add masala paste and turmeric powder to fried onion and cook 3 minutes.

3. Add tomato, blend well and cook 5 minutes.

4. Add mince and salt, blend well and cook till meat water has dried.

5. Add 1½ cups water, bring to the boil, then lower heat and simmer, covered, till mince is cooked.

6. Add vinegar, Worcestershire Sauce and sugar and cook 5 minutes more before removing pan from heat.

7. Serve with potato straws.

Potato Straws (See picture overleaf)

INGREDIENTS

4 medium potatoes weighing
   approximately ½ kg (18 oz)

2 teaspoons salt

Vegetable oil for frying

METHOD

1. Peel potatoes and cut into round wafer-thin slices. Place several slices one on top of another and cut through into very thin strips or straws.

2. Place potato straws in a pan, just cover with water, add salt and keep at least 1 hour.

3. In a "kadai" or wok pour oil to a depth of 5 cm (2 inches) and heat.

4. Drain water from potato straws and add some straws to the hot oil. Do not stir till potato straws reach the surface of oil.

5. Allow to become golden coloured then remove and fry more potato straws. Repeat till all straws are fried.

7. To serve, place mince in middle of platter and surround with potato straws.

❏ Serves 4

40. Masala Liver

Thin slices of liver cooked in a green masala paste.

INGREDIENTS

¼ kg (9 oz) Sheep's liver, cut into long slices

1 onion, finely sliced ⎫
4 cloves garlic
  (½ teaspoon)
1 cm (½ inch) piece of
  fresh ginger root
½ teaspoon cumin seeds ⎬ Grind to a paste
1 medium onion
2 green chillies
2 heaped tablespoons
  roughly chopped
  fresh coriander ⎭

¾ teaspoon salt
2 tablespoons vegetable oil

METHOD

1. Heat oil and fry onion in it till brown. Drain excess oil.
2. Add masala paste and cook 5 minutes adding 2 tablespoons water.
3. Add pieces of liver and fry well 2 minutes.
4. Add ¼ cup water and salt and cook just a few minutes more till liver is cooked.
5. Serve with fried potato chips.

❏ Serves 3

41. Kheema Papetana Pattice

Mince and Potato Patties

Potato patties stuffed with mince, coated in breadcrumbs and fried.

INGREDIENTS

½ kg (18 oz) potato

¾ teaspoon salt (for potatoes)

¼ kg (9 oz) minced mutton

6 cloves garlic

2 cm (1 inch) piece of fresh ginger root

} Grind to a paste (1 teaspoon)

2 tablespoons finely chopped fresh coriander

1 onion, finely sliced

1 green chilli, finely chopped

$1/3$ teaspoon turmeric powder

1 dessertspoon vinegar

1 dessertspoon Worcestershire Sauce

1 dessertspoon sugar

1 teaspoon salt (for mince)

¼ cup dry breadcrumbs

1 egg, slightly beaten

Vegetable oil as required

METHOD

1. Boil potatoes. Peel, then mash till soft and smooth. Add salt and set aside.

2. Fry finely sliced onion in 2 tablespoons oil till brown. Drain excess oil.

3. Add garlic-ginger paste and blend well for 3 minutes.

4. Add coriander, chopped chilli and turmeric powder and continue cooking for 3 more minutes.

5. Add mince and cook till water from mince has evaporated.

6. Add ½ cup water and salt and cook till mince is done and no gravy remains.

7. Mix vinegar, Worcestershire Sauce and sugar in a bowl and add to mince.

8. Continue cooking till vinegar mixture has been absorbed. Keep mince aside and let cool.

9. Divide mashed potato into 6 equal portions. Make each portion into a ball. Place a ball in the palm of the left hand and tap it gently with fingers of right hand flattening it out into a round about 3 inches in diameter.

10. Take about 1 dessertspoon mince and place it in centre of potato round. Fold edges of potato to meet in the centre and completely cover the mince. Seal by pinching potato edges together. Set aside. Do the same with other portions of mashed potato. (If potato sticks to the palm of hand, wet palm first slightly with water).

11. Now roll each potato ball very lightly in breadcrumbs, then in beaten egg and coat again with breadcrumbs. Tap it slightly flat with the blade of a knife and "work" it around with gentle strokes of the knife till it is about 1 cm (½ inch) thick and a perfect round.

12. Shape all potato balls similarly.

13. Pour oil into a frying pan to a depth of 1 cm (½ inch) and heat. Gently place the patties in it and fry till golden brown, turning over once so that both sides are evenly cooked.

14. Serve with fried slices of brinjal (eggplant) (p. 124).

❑ Makes 6 patties

Rice, Curries and Dals

Curry or dal with rice is a perennial favourite for lunch without which, for many, the meal is incomplete. Recipes for these, however, are almost as varied and many as there are cooks. A pinch of this and a pinch of that is added or taken away to suit the taste of an individual or a family, but the basic ingredients remain the same.

Fresh grated coconut or milk of fresh grated coconut is used in the curries. Only if fresh coconut is not available should desiccated coconut be substituted in the masala. But Cream of Coconut (available abroad) has a flavour remarkably similar to milk of fresh coconut which makes it a good substitute.

Now for the accompaniments. Curry and rice is not complete without papadum, kuchumbar and a squeeze of lemon. With a spicy dal, as for Dhansak, kuchumbar and lemon are indispensable and red or white radish a happy addition. With Mori Dal, which is not spiced, goes a generous sprinkling of finely sliced fried onion and ghee or butter.

Further accompaniments are pickles and chutneys. Lime pickle is a favourite and so are carrot pickle and mixed fruit pickle and tomato and mango chutneys. One or more can be served with rice dishes. All these can be bought ready bottled.

Papadum

Papadum (papad) are made from lentils, are wafer thin and light and can be bought in packets. There is a great variety to choose from and you can have your choice from peppered and plain ones, and from those which are to be roasted and others which can be fried.

The roasting variety should be cooked by heating a "tava" or iron griddle to very hot and roasting one side for a minute or two then turning it over to roast the other side.

To fry papadum heat some oil to medium hot in a frying pan or kadai, slide each papadum into it and remove as soon as it is crisp. It will grow in size as it frys and will take only a few seconds to cook. You can also roast the papadum in a microwave oven for one minute on HIGH.

Kuchumbar

Mix together in a small serving bowl 1 large onion, very finely sliced, 2 teaspoons finely chopped fresh coriander, 1 or 2 finely chopped green chillies, 1 dessertspoon vinegar, and 2 teaspoons finely chopped tomato.

42. Dhansak

A favourite for Sunday lunch and one of the best known Parsi dishes,
Dhansak consists of several types of lentils cooked with meat and
vegetables and served with fried brown rice and kavabs.

Dal (Lentils)

INGREDIENTS

½ kg (18 oz) breast or leg of lamb cut into 2½ cm (1 inch) cubes

2 medium onions, finely sliced

6 cloves garlic (¾ teaspoon)

2½ cm (1 inch) piece of fresh ginger root

8 dried red Kashimiri chillies

1 dessertspoon cumin seeds   grind

1 dessertspoon coriander seeds   to a

2½ cm (1 inch piece) cinnamon stick paste

2 cardamoms, peeled   or

4 black peppercorns   use

Paste of 6 cloves garlic and 2½ cm (1 inch) piece fresh ginger root

2 teaspoons Dhansak powder**

2 teaspoons Sambhar powder**

1½ teaspoons turmeric powder

2 teaspoons dhana/jeera powder*

⅓ cup toover dal   Or use 1 cup

⅓ cup moong dal   toover dal

⅓ cup masoor dal   (yellow lentils)

1 medium brinjal (eggplant) cut into 4 pieces

100 g (¼ lb) piece of red pumpkin, peeled and cut into 4 pieces

A few sprigs small leaved methi bhaji (spinach), optional

2 large tomatoes, chopped

1 tablespoon tamarind pulp or 1 teaspoon tamarind concentrate

1 tablespoon jaggery

2½ teaspoons salt

3 tablespoons vegetable oil or melted ghee

* Dhana-jeera powder is a special masala made for Dhansak and is available in stores usually run by Parsis. If you use Dhansak Masala then omit dhana-jeera powder from recipe.

** Mangal's Dhanasak Masala and Sambhar Powder may be used.

METHOD

1. Heat oil in a deep pan and fry onion in it till brown.

2. Add masala paste, turmeric powder and dhana jeera powder and cook 5 minutes.

3. Add tomatoes and cook 5 minutes.

4. Add meat and cook till water from meat has dried.

5. Add the dals, brinjal, tomato and methi bhaji and mix well.

6. Gradually add 6 cups water and salt and bring to the boil. Cover and cook on a low heat till meat is tender. Or pressure cook with 2 cups water. Remove pan from heat.

7. Soak tamarind pulp in $\frac{1}{3}$ cup boiling water for 15 minutes, then strain liquid through a sieve pressing down hard on the tamarind pulp to extract all its juices. Discard pulp.

8. Remove meat from dal and keep aside.

9. Mash dal through a colander into another pan then return meat to dal.

10. Add tamarind juice and jaggery to meat and dal and cook on low heat for 10 minutes adding extra water if dal is too thick.

11. Before serving sprinkle over dal 1 finely sliced onion, fried brown, and ½ dessertspoon finely chopped fresh coriander.

12. Serve with Fried Brown Rice (2 cups) and Kavabs (recipe below) accompanied by Kuchumbar (p. 72) and lemon slices.

❏ Serves 6

Kavabs

INGREDIENTS

½ kg (18 oz) minced mutton

2 medium onions, minced with meat or chopped fine

4 large cloves garlic (¾ teaspoon)

2 cm (¾ inch) piece of ginger root (1 teaspoon)

} Grind to a paste (1 teaspoon)

½ teaspoon turmeric powder

2 tablespoons finely chopped fresh coriander

4 teaspoons finely chopped fresh mint leaves

2 to 4 finely chopped green chillies

2 dessertspoons Worcestershire Sauce

3 medium slices bread

1 egg

1¼ teaspoons salt

½ cup dried breadcrumbs

Vegetable oil for frying

METHOD

1. Soak bread in water for 10 minutes, remove from water and squeeze dry.

2. Mix together all ingredients, except breadcrumbs and oil. Cover and keep 1 hour.

3. Divide mixture into 18 small balls and roll each ball in crumbs till lightly coated all over.

4. In a "kadai" or deep frying pan, pour enough oil for deep-frying and heat to medium hot.

5. Gently fry the kavabs in it till nicely browned.

6. Serve by placing over the rice in serving platter.

Fried Brown Rice

INGREDIENTS

2 cups rice

2 onions, finely sliced

4 teaspoons sugar

2 pieces cinnamon sticks of
   5 cm (2 inches) each

6 cloves

2 teaspoons salt

4 tablespoons vegetable oil

METHOD

1. Soak rice in water for 10 minutes.

2. In a pan heat oil and fry onion in it till brown. Remove pan from heat and drain excess oil.

3. Put sugar in a small pan and brown it over heat till it is very dark brown. Add $1/3$ cup water and cook a few minutes till caramelised sugar has melted. Keep aside.

4. Place pan with fried onion back on heat, drain water from rice and add rice to onion. Cook, stirring frequently, for 3 minutes till rice is nicely fried.

5. Add caramel water and stir till rice is well blended.

6. Add cinnamon stick, cloves, salt and $3^2/3$ cups water. Bring to boil, then cover, lower heat and continue cooking till water is absorbed and rice is cooked.

7. Sprinkle some fried onion over rice before serving.

43. Green Ball Curry

Curry cooked with green masala.
A pleasant variation from the usual "red" curry.

INGREDIENTS

For Kavab Balls

¼ kg (9 oz) minced mutton

2 medium slices bread, soaked in water

1 egg

2 cloves garlic
(¼ teaspoon)

½ cm (¼ inch) piece of
fresh ginger root

} Grind to
a paste
(½ teaspoon)

1 green chilli, finely chopped

1 dessertspoon finely chopped fresh
coriander

½ teaspoon salt

Vegetable oil for frying

For Curry

1 onion, finely sliced

6 cloves garlic (¾ teaspoon)

1 cm (½ inch) piece of
fresh ginger root

4 green chillies

1 teaspoon cumin seeds

1¼ teaspoons turmeric powder

2 tablespoons poppy seeds

$1/3$ teaspoon mustard seeds

2 tablespoons chopped,
fresh coriander

2 tablespoons grated
fresh coconut or
desiccated coconut

} Grind to
a paste

1½ cups milk of ½ coconut* (p. 16)

Juice of ½ lemon (2 teaspoons)

1½ teaspoons salt

2 tablespoons vegetable oil

METHOD

Kavab

1. For the Kavabs, remove bread from water and squeeze dry.

2. Mix together all ingredients for the kavabs, except oil, and keep aside.

* Or use 50 g (about 2 oz) Cream of Coconut with 1½ cups water or use coconut powder
(p. 19).

Curry

1. For the curry, in a pan, heat oil and fry onion in it till pale golden.
2. Add masala paste and blend well. Cook 3 to 4 minutes.
3. Add coconut milk, salt and lemon juice, cover and simmer on low heat for 15 minutes.
4. Add ½ cup water. Continue cooking, covered, for 10 minutes. Remove from heat.
5. Make 12 equal portions of kavab mixture. Roll each portion into a ball.
6. In a "kadai" or deep frying pan, pour oil to a depth of 3½ cm (1½ inches).
7. Fry kavabs in it for 2 minutes then remove and add them to curry mixture.
8. Place pan of curry back on heat and cook, covered, on low heat for 15 to 20 minutes.
9. Remove from heat and serve with White or Yellow Rice (recipes given below) accompanied by Papadum and Kuchumbar (p. 72).

❑ Serves 4

White Rice

INGREDIENTS

1 cup rice

1 teaspoon salt

2 cups water

METHOD

1. Wash rice.
2. In a deep pan add 2 cups water, rice and salt and bring to the boil.
3. Lower heat, cover pan and simmer till all the water has been absorbed. To test if rice is done press a grain of rice to see if it mashes easily. If not quite done, cover pan and allow rice to cook in its own steam without placing the pan back on heat.

Yellow Rice

Cook as for white rice except add ¼ teaspoon turmeric powder and 5 cm (2 inches) piece cinnamon stick to rice when cooking.

44. Chicken Curry

A rich Chicken Curry usually cooked as party fare.

INGREDIENTS

6 cloves garlic (¾ teaspoon)
2 cm (¾ inch) piece of
  fresh ginger root
4 dried, red Kashimiri chillies
1 heaped dessertspoon
  coriander seeds
1 teaspoon cumin seeds
10 black peppercorns
2½ cm (1 inch) piece cinnamon stick
¼ fresh coconut, grated or 2
  tablespoons desiccated coconut

Grind to a paste

1 chicken 1¼ kg (2½ lbs) skinned
  and cut into 8 pieces
2 onions, finely sliced
2 tablespoons poppy seeds
50 g (about 2 oz) cashewnuts
50 g (about 2 oz) sultanas
2 teaspoons salt
2 cups coconut milk from ¾ grated
  fresh coconut* (p. 16)
2 tablespoons cream
4 tablespoons vegetable oil

METHOD

1. Grind poppy seeds, cashewnuts and sultanas each separately.
2. In a pan, heat oil and fry onion in it till brown. Drain excess oil, leaving 1 tablespoon in pan with onion.
3. Add masala paste to onion and mix well. Cook at least 5 minutes adding a little water if masala tends to become too dry.
4. Add ground poppy seeds, cashewnuts and sultanas. Cook 5 minutes more.
5. Add pieces of chicken and fry for 10 minutes in masala stirring occasionally and adding a little water if necessary.
6. Add salt, coconut milk and 2 cups water and cover and cook on low heat till chicken is tender. If curry is too thick add 1 or 2 cups more water and continue simmering a few minutes longer.
7. In case more water is added, taste for salt and add more if necessary.
8. Before serving add cream and simmer 5 minutes.
9. Serve with White Rice (p. 77), Kuchumbar and Papadum (p. 72)

❑ Serves 4

   * Or use 55 g (2 oz) Cream of Coconut and 2 cups water or use coconut powder (p. 19).

45. Mutton Curry

A typical curry in which the spices are ground together with grated fresh coconut.

INGREDIENTS

¼ kg (9 oz) mutton cut into
  2 cm (¾ inch) cubes

2 onions, finely sliced

6 cloves garlic (¾ teaspoon)

2 cm (¾ inch) piece of
  fresh ginger root

4 dried red Kashimiri chillies

2 dessertspoons coriander seeds

1½ teaspoons cumin seeds

1½ teaspoons poppy seeds
  (khus khus)

½ fresh coconut, grated or 4
  tablespoons desiccated coconut

} Grind to a masala paste

1 large tomato, chopped

½ teaspoon turmeric powder

2½ cm (1 inch) piece cinnamon stick

4 cloves

2 potatoes, each cut into 4 pieces

1¾ teaspoons salt

8 curry leaves (curry patta)

4 tablespoons vegetable oil

METHOD

1. Heat oil and fry onion in it till brown. Drain excess oil.
2. Add masala paste and cook 10 minutes, gradually adding ¼ cup water to prevent it from sticking to bottom of pan.
3. Add tomato and blend well. Cover and cook few minutes till tomato is soft.
4. Add meat and cook till water from the meat has dried up.
5. Add turmeric powder, cinnamon stick, cloves, curry patta and salt and blend well for 2 minutes.
6. Add 1 cup water, bring to the boil and simmer, covered 10 minutes.
7. Add 4 more cups water and cook till meat is almost done. Or cook in pressure cooker with 1 cup water.
8. Mix in the potatoes and continue cooking till meat is well cooked.
9. Serve with White Rice (p. 77), Kuchumbar, and Papadum (p. 72) and a generous slice of lemon per person.

❑ Serves 4

46. Papetano Rus

Potato Rus

A popular accompaniment to rice, this Rus which is a special type of curry, is made of potato mashed with coconut milk and added to meat.

INGREDIENTS

½ kg (18 oz) mutton cut into 2 cm (¾ inch) cubes

½ kg (18 oz) potato

3½ cups milk of 1 grated fresh coconut*

2 onions, finely sliced

6 cloves garlic (¾ teaspoon) ⎫
2 cm (¾ inch) piece of fresh ginger root ⎬ Grind to a paste (1½ teaspoons)

2 tablespoons finely chopped fresh coriander

2 green chillies, finely chopped

7 cm (3 inches) piece cinnamon stick

6 cloves

4 cardamoms, shelled

1 teaspoon turmeric powder

1 teaspoon Dhansak masala

3¼ teaspoons salt

4 tablespoons vegetable oil

METHOD

1. Heat meat in a pan until water from the meat has dried. Then gradually add 4 cups water and 1¼ teaspoons salt and simmer, covered, till meat is tender and 1 cup liquid remains. Or pressure cook meat with 1 cup water.

2. Boil potatoes in their jackets, then cool, peel and mash them.

3. Add to mashed potato a little coconut milk at a time, mixing constantly till all the coconut milk has been added. Strain potato mixture through a sieve and set aside. Or mix potato and coconut milk in a blender.

4. In a pan, heat the oil and fry onion in it till golden. Drain excess oil.

5. Add garlic-ginger paste and cook 3 minutes.

6. Add coriander, chillies, cinnamon, cloves, cardamoms, turmeric powder and Dhansak masala and cook 5 minutes.

7. To above mixture add meat and its liquid, mashed potato and 2 teaspoons salt. Bring to the boil then simmer 15 minutes till slightly thickened.

8. Serve with Fried Brown Rice (p. 75), Kuchumber, and Papadum (p. 72).

❑ Serves 4

* Or use 80 g (3 oz) Cream of Coconut mixed with 3½ cups water or use coconut powder (p. 19).

47. Fish Curry

*Although this curry tastes best with Pomfret or Rawas (Indian Salmon),
other white fleshy fish may be substituted for them.*

INGREDIENTS

1 large Pomfret 450 g (1 lb) cut into 6 slices **or** slices of Surmai (Seer) or Rawas (Indian Salmon)

2 large onions, finely sliced

4 to 6 cloves garlic ⎱

½ teaspoon methi seeds (fenugreek seeds)

5 to 6 dried red Kashimiri chillies ⎬ Grind to a paste

3 dessertspoons coriander seeds

½ fresh coconut, grated or 4 tablespoons desiccated coconut ⎰

½ teaspoon turmeric powder

2 cm (¾ inch) piece of fresh ginger root, finely sliced

8 to 10 curry patta (curry leaves)

2 teaspoons salt

2½ cups water

3 tablespoons vegetable oil

Juice of ½ lemon.

METHOD

1. In a deep pan, heat 3 tablespoons oil and fry onion in it gently till onion is just soft but not brown.

2. Remove excess oil, then add masala paste and turmeric powder to onion. Mix well and cook, stirring frequently, for 5 minutes. If necessary, add just enough water during cooking to prevent masala from sticking to bottom of pan.

3. Add sliced ginger and cook 2 minutes. Then add 2½ cups water and curry patta. Cover pan and let mixture simmer for 20 minutes.

4. Add juice of lemon. Add fish and salt and continue cooking till fish is cooked. Serve the fish curry with White Rice (p. 77) accompanied by Kuchumbar and Papadum (p. 72)

❏ Serves 4

48. Fish Pilau

Fish Pilau can be prepared in several ways.
Here is one which has the exotic aroma of traditional ingredients.

INGREDIENTS

1 large Pomfret (450 g or 1 lb) cut into 2½ cm (1 inch) thick slices

1 cup rice

4 onions, finely sliced

10 cloves garlic (1¼ teaspoons) ⎫
10 dried red Kashmiri chillies ⎬ Grind to a paste
1 teaspoon cumin seeds ⎭

½ cup yoghurt

½ teaspoon pure saffron

Juice of ½ lemon

2 teaspoons salt

Vegetable oil as required

METHOD

1. Soak saffron in lemon juice.

2. To 6 cups boiling water add rice and I teaspoon salt. Continue boiling rice till it is half cooked. Drain water and keep rice aside.

3. In 6 tablespoons oil fry onion till deep golden. Remove ¾ of the fried onion and set aside.

4. Drain excess oil from remaining onion leaving 1 tablespoon oil in pan, then add masala paste to onion in pan and blend well.

5. Add fish and 1 teaspoon salt and mix well.

6. Add 2 tablespoons water and cook 5 minutes. Remove pan from heat and set aside.

7. Mix ½ reserved onion and yoghurt into rice. Spread rice over fish.

8. Sprinkle lemon juice and saffron mixture over rice. Sprinkle remaining fried onion over rice.

9. Pour 2 tablespoons oil over rice.

10. Cover pan tightly and place in moderately hot oven till rice is cooked.

11. Turn out into a platter and serve with Curry Gravy (p. 93), Curry Sauce (p. 94) or Curd (Yoghurt) Curry (p. 89).

❑ Serves 6

49. Fish Molee

*A fish curry of gentle flavour made of coconut milk and
tinted green with fresh green chillies.*

INGREDIENTS

1 large Pomfret 400 g (about 1 lb) cut into
  2 cm (¾ inch) thick slices

1 medium onion, chopped fine

6 cloves garlic (¾ teaspoon) ⎤

3 green chillies

½ teaspoon cumin seeds

2 tablespoons poppy seeds   ⎬ Grind to
                                 a paste
1 teaspoon turmeric powder

¼ grated fresh coconut or
  2 tablespoons desiccated
  coconut   ⎦

2 cups milk from ¾ grated coconut (p 16)*

1½ teaspoons salt

1 extra whole green chilli

Juice of 1 lemon (1 tablespoon)

2 tablespoons vegetable oil

METHOD

1. In a pan, heat the oil and fry onion in it till onion is soft but not brown. Drain excess oil.

2. Add masala paste to onion and cook 5 minutes.

3. Add ½ cup water and cook 3 minutes.

4. Add coconut milk and salt. Bring mixture to the boil and boil 2 minutes.

5. Add fish. Bring mixture to the boil again, then lower heat, add 1 whole green chilli, and simmer, covered, till fish is cooked.

6. When ready add lemon juice.

7. Serve as a curry with White Rice (p. 77), Kuchumbar and Papadum (p. 72) or as an independent dish to be eaten with bread.

❑ Serves 4

  * Or use 55 g (2 oz) Cream of Coconut plus 2 cups water or use coconut powder (p. 19).

50. Dhan-Dal Patio

A meal in itself, this dish of white rice, lentils and fish patio is traditionally eaten on festive occasions and "good" days. It is sufficiently a favourite, however, to be enjoyed more often even on ordinary days.

INGREDIENTS

For the Mori Dal (Lentils)

1 cup toover dal (soaked in water for 2 hours)

$1/3$ teaspoon turmeric powder

1 teaspoon salt

4 cups water

5 tablespoons vegetable oil

2 onions, finely sliced

2 or 3 cloves garlic, finely chopped

For the Patio

1 Pomfret weighing 400 g (14 oz) cut into 6 slices or slices of Surmai (Seer) or Rawas (Indian Salmon)

2 large onions, finely sliced

6 cloves garlic (¾ teaspoon) ⎫
4 dried red Kashimiri chillies ⎬ Grind to a paste
1½ teaspoons cumin seeds ⎭

½ teaspoon turmeric powder

3 tablespoons finely chopped fresh coriander

1 teaspoon Dhansak masala

2 large tomatoes, chopped

1 tablespoon tamarind pulp or 1 teaspoon tamarind concentrate

1 tablespoon jaggery (gur)

1 large brinjal (eggplant) cut into 8 pieces

2 teaspoons salt

3 tablespoons vegetable oil

METHOD

Mori Dal

1. Drain water from dal. Boil dal in 4 cups water adding turmeric powder and salt. When soft, mash dal through a strainer.

2. Fry finely sliced onions in 5 tablespoons oil till golden brown.

3. Remove half fried onion together with half the oil into a bowl.

4. Add finely chopped garlic to remaining onion and continue frying till garlic is well fried and golden.

5. Add dal to onion garlic mixture and mix well.

84

Patio

1. Fry onion in 3 tablespoons oil till brown.

2. Add masala paste and turmeric powder and cook for 5 minutes till well blended. Add 1 dessertspoon water if masala tends to stick to bottom of pan.

3. Add coriander and Dhansak masala and cook 2 minutes.

4. Add tomatoes, blend well and cook 5 minutes.

5. Add 1½ cups water and salt and let mixture simmer, covered, 5 minutes.

6. Soak tamarind in $^1/_3$ cup boiling water for 15 minutes, then strain liquid through a sieve pressing down hard on the tamarind pulp to extract all its juice. Discard pulp.

7. Add tamarind juice and jaggery to main mixture and continue cooking, covered, 5 minutes more.

8. Add brinjal and when brinjal is half-cooked, add fish and continue cooking till fish is done.

9. To serve oneself, White Rice (p. 77) should be taken first, the dal should then be poured over the rice and over it all should be the fish patio. Heat the reserved fried onion in oil and serve separately in a bowl. About I teaspoon per serving should be poured over the patio in each plate.

❑ Serves 4

51. Prawn Curry

Since prawns (shrimps) are not available throughout the year,
and especially during the monsoon season,
this popular curry features often in the day's menu when prawns can be easily purchased.

INGREDIENTS

25 prawns or shrimps, shelled, cleaned and deveined

1 onion, finely sliced

6 dried red Kashimiri chillies

4 to 6 cloves garlic

1 dessertspoon coriander seeds

1 tablespoon grated coconut

1 cup milk from ½ fresh grated coconut*

½ teaspoon turmeric powder

2 teaspoons lemon juice

1¾ teaspoons salt

2 tablespoons vegetable oil

METHOD

1. Grind to a paste the chillies, garlic, coriander seeds and 1 tablespoon grated coconut.

2. In a pan, heat oil and fry onion in it till pale gold. Remove onion and set aside.

3. In same oil fry the masala paste and turmeric powder for 10 minutes, adding a little water if necessary.

4. Add fried onion and prawns to masala paste and blend well.

5. Add 1¼ cups water and salt and cook till prawns are nearly cooked.

6. Add lemon juice and coconut milk to nearly cooked prawns and continue cooking till prawns are done.

7. Serve with White Rice (p. 77) accompanied with Papadum and Kuchumbar (p. 72).

❑ Serves 4

* Or use 50 g (2 oz) Cream of Coconut plus 1 cup water or use Coconut powder (p. 19).

52. Meat Pilau

*Curried meat and saffron rice are cooked separately and
then baked together for a rich and delicious mingling of flavours.*

INGREDIENTS:

½ kg (18 oz) mutton cut into
  3 cm (1¼ inch) cubes

6 tablespoons vegetable oil

4 onions, finely sliced

4 dried red Kashimiri chillies ⎤

1¼ teaspoons cumin seeds   ⎬ Grind
masala to
6 cloves garlic (¾ teaspoon)   a paste*

2 cm (¾ inch) piece
  fresh ginger root ⎦

2 cardamoms, peeled ⎤
4 cloves   ⎬ Powdered
4 black peppercorns ⎦

3½ teaspoons salt

2 large potatoes, peeled and cut into
  4 pieces each

2 cups rice, soaked in water 10 minutes

2 tablespoons kismis (seedless raisins)

1 teaspoon pure saffron

Juice of 1 lemon

3 tablespoons yoghurt

METHOD

1. Heat oil in a pan and fry onion in it till brown. Drain excess oil.

2. Remove half the onion and keep aside.

3. In the remaining onion, add the masala paste and blend well. Cook 5 minutes, then add powdered spices (cardamom, cloves and peppercorns). Cook 5 minutes, adding a little water if masala tends to stick to bottom of pan.

4. Add meat and cook till water from the meat has dried up.

5. Add 1 cup warm water and 1½ teaspoons salt and simmer 20 minutes.

6. Add 2 more cups warm water and continue simmering.

7. When meat is nearly done, add 1 more cup warm water, if necessary, and continue cooking till meat is tender and 1½ cups gravy remains. Or pressure cook meat with 1½ cups water.

  * Or use 1½ teaspoons Mangal's Red Chilli, Jeera And Garlic Paste.

8. Soak saffron in lemon juice.

9. Boil rice in 4 cups water with 2 teaspoons salt.

10. Boil potatoes in water for 1 minute. Remove, then fry them in 1 cm (½ inch) oil till they are cooked. Remove and keep aside.

11. Fry the kismis and keep aside.

12. Divide rice into 3 equal portions.

13. In a deep pan, pour 1 tablespoon oil.

14. Mix saffron and lemon juice mixture into 1 portion of rice and place it in bottom of pan.

15. Over this spread half of meat mixture and gravy.

16. Divide second portion of rice into 2 equal parts.

17. Spread one part over meat mixture in pan.

18. Over this sprinkle half of reserved fried onion and all the fried potatoes.

19. Cover with second part of divided second portion of rice.

20. Over this, place remaining meat and gravy.

21. Mix 3 tablespoons curd into third portion of rice and spread it over meat mixture. Pour 1 tablespoon oil over it, cover pan and place in medium hot oven for ½ hour to heat through.

22. To serve, spoon rice into a platter and sprinkle remaining fried onion and fried kismis over rice. Serve with Curd (Yoghurt) Curry (p. 89).

23. Or to give the rice a different festivel look, layer the rice and meat as mentioned above into a large ring mould, reserving a quarter portion of the meat mixture. Overturn the ring mould in a serving dish and place the reserved portion of meat in the centre of the ring mould.

❏ Serves 6

Facing page—Meat Pilau (page 87),
Overleaf—Dhansak (page 73)

53. Curd (Yoghurt) Curry

This light curry is especially suited to accompany rice which is cooked with meat, fish or vegetables like Pilaus, Byrianis and rich Khichdees.

INGREDIENTS

2 cups yoghurt

2 onions, finely sliced

4 cloves garlic, finely chopped

2 green chillies, finely chopped

¼ teaspoon cumin seeds

$^1/_3$ teaspoon turmeric powder

1½ tablespoons finely chopped fresh coriander

1 teaspoon salt

1 tablespoon vegetable oil

METHOD

1. In a pan, heat oil and fry onion in it till golden.

2. Add garlic, chillies, cumin seeds, turmeric powder and coriander and cook 3 minutes.

3. Mix salt in yoghurt and add to onion mixture.

4. Lower heat and heat mixture slowly. Remove from heat before it comes to the boil.

5. Serve at once.

   (Onion mixture can be kept ready before hand and the yoghurt added and heated just before serving.)

❑ Serves 4 to 6

Previous page—Meat with Apricots (page 60),
Facing page—Kheema Papetana Pattice (page 70)

54. Tomato Rice

Rice cooked in tomato juice.

INGREDIENTS

2 cups rice, soaked in water ½ hour

1 kg (2 lbs) ripe, red tomatoes

3 to 4 cloves garlic, slightly crushed

3 cloves, slightly crushed

5 cm (2 inches) piece cinnamon stick

3 black peppercorns

2 onions, quartered

4 teaspoons sugar

1 dessertspoon Worcestershire Sauce

1 tablespoon butter

2 tablespoons finely chopped onion

4 teaspoons salt

METHOD

1. Cut tomatoes in halves; put in a pan with garlic, cloves, cinnamon, peppercorns, 2 onions, quartered, 1 cup water and 2 teaspoons salt. Cook till tomatoes are very soft.

2. Mash tomatoes through a strainer into another pan. Discard pulp.

3. Add Worcestershire Sauce and sugar to tomatoes and cook 5 minutes.

4. In another pan, heat butter and fry 2 tablespoons chopped onion in it till onion is pale gold.

5. Strain rice, add to onion and fry 10 minutes, stirring frequently.

6. To the rice add tomato juice and water to make 4 cups liquid. Add 2 teaspoons salt and cook, covered, on low heat till rice is cooked. Serve with Boti-Soti (p. 46) or Chicken with Cashewnuts (p. 43).

❑ Serves 4 to 6

55. Vegetable Khichdee

A rich rice recipe—rice and lentils with mixed vegetables and spices cooked together in coconut milk.

INGREDIENTS

2 cups rice, soaked in water ½ hour

½ cup masoor dal, (red lentils) cleaned and soaked in water 1 hour

4 onions, finely sliced

1 onion, roughly chopped

100 g (4 oz) potato, peeled and cut into small cubes

100 g (4 oz) carrots, scraped and cut into small cubes

100 g (4 oz) bhindi (okra) cut into ½ cm (¼ inch) rounds

6 cloves garlic (¾ teaspoon) ⎤

2 cm (¾ inch) piece of fresh ginger root ⎬ Grind to a paste (1 teaspoon)

¾ teaspoon Dhansak masala ⎦

1 teaspoon turmeric powder

¾ teaspoon cumin seeds

4 cardamoms, shelled and powdered (¼ teaspoon)

10 cloves

6 black peppercorns

4 tablespoons fresh coriander, finely chopped

4 green chillies, finely chopped

7 cm (3 inches) piece cinnamon stick

¼ fresh coconut, grated

3 cups milk from ¾ grated fresh coconut*

4¼ teaspoons salt

Vegetable oil as required.

METHOD

1. In a pan, heat 6 tablespoons oil and fry 4 onions, finely sliced, in it till golden. Remove excess oil. Remove 1 tablespoon onion and keep aside.

2. In a frying pan, heat 3 tablespoons oil and fry potatoes. Remove and set aside. In the same oil, fry carrots and set aside, then fry the bhindi and set aside.

3. Mix all vegetables together and add ¾ teaspoon salt to them.

4. To the fried onion, add garlic-ginger paste and cook 5 minutes.

   * Or use 85 g (3 oz) Cream of Coconut and 3 cups water or coconut powder (p. 19).

5. Now add Dhansak Masala, turmeric powder, cumin seeds, cardamoms, cloves, peppercorns, coriander, chillies, grated coconut and cinnamon stick and cook 5 to 7 minutes.

6. Add rice, dal, 1 chopped onion and 3½ teaspoons salt and cook at least 5 minutes, stirring frequently.

7. Add vegetables, coconut milk and water to make up 4 cups of liquid, and cook, covered, till almost all the liquid has been absorbed. Then put pan, covered, into a medium hot oven till all the liquid is absorbed and rice and dal are cooked.

8. Serve sprinkled with reserved fried onion, and accompanied by Curd (Yoghurt) Curry (p. 89), Kuchumbar and Papadum (p. 72).

❏ Serves 4

56. Curry Gravy

A spiced gravy to serve with Pilau or Khichdee.

INGREDIENTS

1 onion, finely sliced

¼ fresh coconut, grated, or
   2 tablespoons desiccated
   coconut

3 cloves garlic ($^1/_3$ teaspoon)

1 cm (½ inch) piece of
   fresh ginger root

1 teaspoon poppy seeds

¾ teaspoon cumin seeds

3 teaspoons coriander seeds

} Grind to
a paste

½ teaspoon turmeric powder

1 small tomato chopped

1 teaspoon salt

2 tablespoons oil

METHOD

1. Heat oil in a pan and fry onion in it till brown. Drain excess oil.

2. Add masala paste and turmeric powder to onion and cook 5 minutes adding a little water if mixture sticks to bottom of pan.

3. Add tomato and cook 2 minutes.

4. Gradually add 2 cups water and salt and simmer, covered, for 20 minutes.

5. If gravy is too thick add ½ to 1 cup more water and continue cooking 5 to 10 minutes longer.

6. Serve with rice, especially Khichdee, Pilau and any other rice which has meat or fish cooked with it.

❑ Serves 4

57. Curry Sauce

*A simple curry sauce to make when cooking abroad - made with
curry powder and Cream of Coconut.*

INGREDIENTS

1 onion, finely sliced

1½ teaspoons curry powder

2 dessertspoons flour

4 green chillies, slit

2 cups soup stock made with meat bones or
with 2 chicken or meat soup cubes

2 cups water

1 teaspoon salt

2 dessertspoons lemon juice

55g (2 oz) Cream of Coconut

2 tablespoons vegetable oil or other
cooking medium.

METHOD

1. In a pan, heat oil and fry sliced onion in it till brown.

2. Add curry powder and mix well adding 1 tablespoon water.

3. Mix a little water into the flour to make a paste and add to onion mixture.

4. Gradually add 1 cup water then add Cream of Coconut. Allow it to melt and blend well.

5. Add green chillies, stock, salt and lemon juice and cook on low heat 10 minutes.

6. Add 1 more cup water if necessary, allow to boil 5 minutes then remove from heat.

7. Serve with Pilaus, Tomato Rice (p. 90) or Vegetable Khichdee (p. 91) or add boiled
   pieces of meat and serve as Meat Curry with White Rice (p. 77).

❑ Serves 4

Eggs

To Parsis, eggs are not merely a breakfast food. An egg dish can form an important and very popular part of a menu for lunch or dinner and is usually served as a first course.

Since repetition of a menu is not appreciated, different ways of preparing eggs are a challenge well worth taking on. The result is egg dishes difficult to compare for variety and taste and, what is more, highly decorative as well.

58. Picnic Poro

Picnic Omelette

*A filling omelette with potatoes, onions and
a touch of spice blended into the eggs.*

INGREDIENTS

2 eggs

½ teaspoon cumin seeds

1 tablespoon finely chopped
fresh coriander

1 or 2 green chillies

⎱ Grind to
⎰ a paste

1 medium potato, peeled and cut into tiny
cubes

1 medium onion, finely chopped

½ teaspoon salt

3 tablespoons vegetable oil

METHOD

1. Cook potato cubes for 1 minute in boiling water. Strain and cool slightly.

2. In a 20 cm (8-inch) frying pan heat oil and fry potatoes in it a few minutes till cooked.
   Remove and set aside.

3. Separate eggs and beat egg whites till soft peaks form. Add yolks and continue beating
   till well blended.

4. Add masala paste to eggs and blend well with a fork in a "beating" motion.

5. Add onion, potato cubes and salt and blend thoroughly.

6. Reheat oil in frying pan and when hot pour egg mixture into it. Reduce heat to
   medium, cover and cook till bottom layer of omelette is brown. Turn omelette over
   and cook other side till brown.

7. Cut into 4 portions and serve each portion between two slices of plain or buttered
   bread.

59. Parsi Poro

Parsi Omelette

A breakfast omelette.

INGREDIENTS

1 egg

2 teaspoons very finely chopped onion

2 teaspoons very finely chopped fresh coriander

1 green chilli, finely chopped

¼ teaspoon salt

¼ tablespoon vegetable oil

METHOD

1. Heat oil in a 15 cm (6-inch) frying pan.

2. Separate egg and beat egg white till soft peaks form.

3. Add egg yolk and continue beating till well blended.

4. Add onion, coriander, chilli and salt and mix well.

5. Pour mixture into medium hot oil and cover and cook on medium heat till lower layer of omelette is nicely browned.

6. Turn omelette over carefully and cook other side, uncovered, till it is also brown.

7. Make separately, as many omelettes as desired.

60. Egg Vindaloo

*These spicy eggs form an unusual variation of Vindaloo
which is usually made with meats.*

INGREDIENTS

4 large onions, finely sliced

4 eggs

3 dried red Kashimiri chillies ⎫
6 cloves garlic (¾ teaspoon) ⎬ Grind to a paste
¾ teaspoon cumin seeds ⎭

1 dessertspoon Worcestershire Sauce

1 dessertspoon vinegar

¾ dessertspoon sugar

1½ teaspoons salt

8 tablespoons vegetable oil

METHOD

1. Add eggs into boiling water and boil for 8 minutes till eggs are hard-boiled.

2. Peel and carefully cut away the whites of eggs so that the yolks remain whole. Cut whites of eggs into very thin slices.

3. In a pan, heat the oil and add onion. Fry till onion is soft but not brown. Drain excess oil leaving 2 tablespoons in onion.

4. To the onion, add the masala paste and cook 5 minutes.

5. Add Worcestershire Sauce, vinegar and sugar and cook 5 minutes.

6. Add ½ cup water and continue cooking 5 minutes more.

7. Add salt and whites of eggs and blend well. Cook, covered, on low heat, for 5 to 10 minutes. Add yolks of eggs but do not mix as the yolks might break. Cover and cook 2 or 3 minutes longer before serving.

❑ Serves 4

61. Beaten Eggs on Potato

Thin slices of potato cooked with onion and spices,
topped with frothy, beaten eggs and baked.

INGREDIENTS

½ kg (18 oz) potatoes (4 large)

¼ kg (9 oz) onions (2 large), finely sliced

2 green chillies, finely chopped

2 tablespoons finely chopped fresh
coriander

1 teaspoon salt

2 eggs

3 tablespoons oil

METHOD

1. Peel potatoes and cut into thin slices less than ¼ cm ($^1/_8$-inch) thick. If slices are too large, cut them into halves or even quarters so that no side of a potato slice is more than 2½ cm (1 inch) long. (The shape does not matter.)

2. In a frying pan, heat oil and fry onion till golden. Remove some oil.

3. Add chillies, coriander and salt and blend well. Cook on low heat for 5 minutes.

4. Add potatoes and blend well a few minutes. Add ¼ cup water and cover and cook 5 minutes. Add ¼ cup more water then cover again and continue cooking. Stir mixture frequently to prevent it from sticking to bottom of pan, adding a little water whenever necessary. Cook till potatoes are soft.

5. Spread mixture evenly in frying pan, preferably a non-stick frying pan, or remove to a 23 cm (9-inch) pie plate.

6. Separate eggs. Beat egg whites till soft peaks form.

7. Add egg yolks and blend.

8. Pour beaten eggs over potato mixture and spread evenly over surface.

9. If mixture is in a frying pan, cover and cook on low heat till eggs are set. If mixture is in a pie plate, bake in a moderately hot oven till eggs are firm.

❑ Serves 4

62. Akoori

*Akoori eggs are good for Sunday breakfast and may also be served
on toast as a savoury and
on biscuits or bite-size pieces of toast as cocktail eats.*

INGREDIENTS

4 eggs

2 medium onions, finely chopped

2 tablespoons finely chopped fresh
coriander

2 green chillies, finely chopped (optional)

1 medium tomato, finely chopped

¾ teaspoon salt

3 tablespoons vegetable oil

METHOD

1. Heat oil and fry onion in it till soft but not brown. Remove excess oil.

2. Add coriander, chillies and tomato and blend well. Cook 3 minutes. Remove pan from heat.

3. Break eggs into a bowl and beat with a few strokes till whites and yolks are well blended.

4. Add to onion mixture and mix well.

5. Add salt.

6. Return pan to heat and cook, slowly stirring all the time, till mixture is consistency of soft scrambled eggs.

❑ Serves 2 to 3

63. Bhindi-Eggs

Eggs on Okra

*Frothy, beaten eggs evenly spread over chopped
bhindi (okra) and onion mixture.*

INGREDIENTS

2 large onions, roughly chopped

3 tablespoons vegetable oil

¼ kg (9 oz) bhindi (okra) sliced into ½ cm
(¼ inch) rounds

½ teaspoon chilli powder

$^1/_3$ teaspoon turmeric powder

½ teaspoon salt

2 eggs

METHOD

1. In a frying pan (preferably non-stick) heat the oil and fry onion till pale golden in colour. Drain excess oil.

2. Add chilli powder and turmeric powder and blend well. Cook 2 minutes.

3. Add bhindi and mix well. Add salt, cover and cook on low heat for 5 minutes. Remove lid and stir to make sure the vegetable is not sticking to the pan. In case it is sticking, sprinkle some water over it.

4. Cover and cook another 5 minutes. Check again and sprinkle more water, if necessary.

5. Cover and cook another 5 minutes or till vegetable is cooked.

6. Separate egg whites from yolks and beat egg whites till frothy and soft peaks form.

7. Mix egg yolks lightly with fork (just a few strokes) then blend into beaten whites.

8. Spread evenly over vegetable mixture in frying pan, preferably a non-stick frying pan. Cover and cook on low heat till eggs are set.

9. Or put vegetable mixture into a 20 cm (8-inch) pie plate or shallow baking dish and spread egg mixture evenly over it. Bake in a moderately hot oven till eggs are set.

10. Divide into 4 portions and serve at once.

❏ Serves 4

64. Sali Pur Eeda

Eggs on Potato Straws

Whole eggs on potato straws cooked gently on low heat or baked.

INGREDIENTS

Potato straws made from 4 medium
  potatoes weighing approximately ½ kg
  (p. 67)

4 eggs

METHOD

1. Spread potato straws evenly in a large frying pan (preferably non-stick).
2. Pour 8 tablespoons water evenly over the potato straws and cook on low heat till water has evaporated and potato straws are soft.
3. Break 4 eggs over the potato straws keeping eggs whole as for fried eggs.
4. Cover and cook on low heat till eggs are set. Or put sali into a pie plate, place whole eggs over it and bake in a moderate oven and serve when eggs are set.

❏ Serves 4

65. Sweet Omelette

Beaten eggs blended with sugar makes this sweet omelette
which can be served at breakfast.

INGREDIENTS

2 eggs

2 tablespoons milk

2 teaspoons sugar

1 tablespoon butter

METHOD

1. Break eggs into a bowl and beat till light and frothy.

2. Add milk and sugar and beat with a few strokes more to blend well.

3. Heat butter in a 20 cm (8-inch) frying pan and when hot pour egg mixture into it spreading it evenly in the frying pan.

4. Cook on low heat till bottom layer of omelette is golden brown, then turn omelette over and allow other side to cook golden brown. Serve at once.

66. Prawn Omelettes

Omelettes stuffed with prawns or shrimps.

INGREDIENTS

15 large prawns, shelled and cleaned

4 cloves garlic (½ teaspoon) ⎤

1 green chilli   ⎥ Grind to

2½ heaped tablespoons   ⎥ a paste

   chopped fresh coriander

½ teaspoon tamarind ⎦

½ tablespoon vegetable oil

4 eggs

2 medium onions, finely chopped

2 medium tomatoes, finely chopped

2½ teaspoons salt

4 tablespoons melted butter

METHOD

1. In a pan, heat oil. Fry masala paste in it for 5 minutes, adding 1 tablespoon water if necessary.

2. Add prawns and fry for a few minutes, then add ¼ cup water and ½ teaspoon salt and simmer, covered, till prawns are cooked and water has evaporated.

3. Separate 2 eggs.

4. Beat egg whites till soft peaks form.

5. Add yolks and continue beating till well blended.

6. Add half the onions and tomatoes. Add 1 teaspoon salt and blend well.

7. In a 20 cm (8-inch) frying pan heat 2 tablespoons butter.

8. When hot, pour egg mixture into it and cover and cook on low heat till bottom layer of omelette is golden brown and the upper layer firm to the touch.

9. Heat prawns and spread half the amount on one half of omelette. Fold other half of omelette over mixture and remove from pan.

10. Make another similar omelette with remaining 2 eggs.

❑ Makes 2 omelettes

67. Eggs on Onion, Coriander and Tomato

Beaten eggs spread over gently spiced
mixed vegetables and baked.

INGREDIENTS

2 eggs

½ kg (18 oz) onion, finely sliced

6 cloves garlic

4 green chillies   } Grind to a paste

1 teaspoon cumin seeds

2 cups lightly packed finely chopped fresh coriander

¼ kg (9 oz) tomatoes, chopped

2 teaspoons sugar

2 teaspoons lemon juice

1 teaspoon salt

Vegetable oil as required

METHOD

1. Heat enough oil in a large frying pan to fry the onions. Fry till soft and pale gold, not dark. Remove any excess oil.

2. Add masala paste to onion and fry 2 or 3 minutes.

3. Add coriander, tomatoes and salt and mix well. Cook 10 minutes.

4. Add sugar and lemon juice and mix well.

5. Separate eggs and beat egg whites till soft peaks form. Add yolks and continue beating till well blended.

6. Spread onion mixture evenly in frying pan and pour beaten eggs over it spreading evenly over mixture.

7. Cover and cook on low heat till eggs are set.

8. Or put onion mixture into 20 cm (8-inch) pie plate, spread beaten eggs over it and bake in moderately hot oven till eggs are set.

9. Cut into 4 portions and serve at once.

❑ Serves 4

68. Baked Eggs on Cream

Baked eggs on cream make an appetizing first course to any meal.

INGREDIENTS

4 eggs

2 teaspoons butter

4 large cloves garlic, finely sliced

1 green chilli, seeded and finely chopped

8 tablespoons thick cream

$1/3$ teaspoon salt

METHOD

1. Heat butter and fry garlic and chilli in it a few minutes. Garlic should not turn brown.
2. Add cream, blend well and cook 2 minutes.
3. Pour mixture into a pie plate, sprinkle with salt and allow to cool.
4. 20 minutes before serving break eggs on to cream mixture and place in hot oven till eggs are firm.

❑ Serves 4

69. Scrambled Eggs with Raisins

Sweetened scrambled eggs.

INGREDIENTS

4 eggs

4 teaspoons seedless raisins (kismis)

1 small onion, finely chopped

4 dessertspoons milk

2 dessertspoons water

¾ teaspoon salt

2 dessertspoons melted butter

METHOD

1. In a pan, heat butter and fry raisins in it 1 or 2 minutes. Remove and keep aside.

2. To the same butter add onion and cook till just soft. Remove from heat.

3. In a bowl, break the eggs and blend well. Add milk, water and salt, mix well and add to onion.

4. Cook on low heat and keep stirring slowly till eggs are half scrambled.

5. Add raisins and continue cooking till eggs are properly scrambled, but soft.

6. Serve at once.

❑ Makes 2 servings

70. Eggs on Spinach

Spinach cooked with spices makes a tasty base for beaten eggs.

INGREDIENTS

1 kg (2 lbs) cholai bhaji (spinach)

2 medium onions, finely sliced

4 cloves garlic (½ teaspoon)

½ inch piece of fresh ginger root

1 or 2 green chillies

} Grind to a paste

½ teaspoon turmeric powder

½ teaspoon chilli powder

½ cup finely chopped fresh coriander

2 teaspoons Worcestershire Sauce

1½ teaspoons sugar

1 teaspoons salt

2 tablespoons vegetable oil

2 eggs

METHOD

1. Clean spinach by plucking the leaves and tender stalks and discarding the thick stalks. Wash leaves, then chop them.

2. In a pan, heat oil and fry onion in it till pale yellow.

3. Add chilli paste and cook 3 minutes.

4. Add turmeric powder, chilli powder and coriander and cook 3 minutes more.

5. Add spinach, blend well, add salt then cover and cook on low heat 10 minutes.

6. Add Worcestershire Sauce and sugar and continue cooking on low heat a few minutes more till spinach is cooked. Cook uncovered till most of the liquid has dried.

7. Separate eggs and beat whites of eggs till soft peaks form. Add yolks and blend.

8. Put spinach in a 20 cm (8-inch) pie plate, spread beaten eggs over surface of spinach and bake in a moderately hot oven till eggs are set and golden.

9. Serve at once.

❑ Serves 4

71. Eggs on Tomato

Baked eggs on tomato makes a substantial and decorative first course to a meal.

INGREDIENTS

½ kg (18 oz) tomatoes

1 onion, finely sliced

1 onion, finely chopped

2 cloves garlic (¼ teaspoon)

½ cm (¼ inch) piece fresh ginger root

$^1/_3$ teaspoon turmeric powder

½ teaspoon chilli powder

1 tablespoon finely chopped fresh coriander

½ teaspoon salt

1 dessertspoon vinegar

1 dessertspoon sugar

4 eggs

2 tablespoons vegetable oil

METHOD

1. Boil tomatoes in 2 cups water a few minutes till tomatoes are slightly soft.

2. Remove tomatoes, cool, then peel and chop roughly.

3. In a frying pan, heat the oil, then fry 1 finely sliced onion in it till golden.

4. Grind garlic and ginger to a paste, add to fried onion and cook 2 minutes.

5. Add turmeric powder, chilli powder, coriander and chopped onion and blend well. Cook 2 minutes.

6. Add tomato pulp and salt and cook, uncovered, till mixture is almost dry.

7. Add vinegar and sugar and continue cooking till liquid has almost evaporated.

8. Put tomato mixture into a pie plate and with the back of a spoon make 4 evenly spaced out hollows in the mixture.

9. Break an egg into each hollow, place in medium hot oven and bake till eggs are set.

❑ Serves 4

Vegetarian

Although essentially non-vegetarian, Parsi cooking also includes vegetarian dishes which are imaginative and interesting and have taste-appeal for all palates.

72. Chutney-Stuffed Brinjals

(Eggplant)

This is a tasty and substantial way of serving brinjals (eggplant or aubergine).

INGREDIENTS

1 kg (2¼ lbs) medium sized brinjals

2 tablespoons vegetable oil

½ cup water

Green Chutney (p. 21)

METHOD

1. Cut brinjals down middle without cutting right through. Cut again at right angles to the first cut so that each brinjal is divided into quarters.

2. Make Green Chutney as on page 21 but increase salt to 1½ teaspoons.

3. Fill the chutney between sections of each brinjal then "close" up the brinjal again as tightly as possible.

4. In a pan, heat the oil and fry brinjals in it for a minute or two turning them so that they are coated all over with oil.

5. Add ½ cup water, cover and simmer 15 minutes.

6. If water has dried up in 15 minutes, add more water and continue simmering till the brinjals are tender.

7. Serve with Mutton or Fish Cutlets, (p. 24) Crumb-Fried Lamb Chops, (p. 47) Mince and Potato Patties (p. 70) or as an individual vegetable dish with Potato Straws (p. 67).

❑ Serves 4 to 6

73. Fried Bananas

*A favourite with Parsis, served as an accompaniment to almost any dish,
especially "dry" dishes like cutlets and chops or with mince.*

INGREDIENTS

6 red or yellow skinned cooking bananas

Vegetable oil for frying

METHOD

1. If bananas are not very soft, soften them by rolling hard on a flat surface before peeling.
2. Peel bananas and cut into 3 cm (1¼ inches) slices.
3. Pour oil to a depth of 5 cm (2 inches) in a "kadai", wok-shaped pan or deep frying pan. Heat to boiling.
4. Add to oil as many pieces of banana as will fit easily into the "kadai." Lower heat to medium and cover and fry 5 minutes.
5. Uncover and continue frying till bananas are soft and deep golden brown.
6. Remove and set aside and fry remaining pieces.

❑ 4 to 6 servings

74. Red Pumpkin Patio

*This sweet, sour and spicy red pumpkin dish can be served
as a vegetable or as an accompaniment to rice.*

INGREDIENTS

½ kg (18 oz) red pumpkin

6 cloves garlic (¾ teaspoon) ⎫
2 teaspoons cumin seeds   ⎬ Grind to
3 dried red Kashimiri chillies ⎪ a paste
1 medium onion   ⎭

1 large onion, finely sliced

¾ teaspoon salt

2 teaspoons lemon juice

1 teaspoon sugar

1 dessertspoon finely chopped fresh
  coriander

2 tablespoons vegetable oil

METHOD

1. Remove skin and seeds from red pumpkin and cut pumpkin into 2 cm (¾ inch) squares.

2. In a pan, heat oil and fry sliced onion in it till soft but not brown.

3. Add masala paste and cook 5 minutes.

4. Add pieces of pumpkin, salt and $1/3$ cup water, bring to the boil, then cover and cook on low heat till pumpkin is very tender.

5. Remove pan from heat and mash pumpkin.

6. Return pan to heat, add lemon juice and sugar and simmer gently 5 minutes.

7. Turn out into dish, sprinkle with fresh coriander and serve with White Rice (p. 77) and Mori Dal (p. 84) or with cutlets or chops as an accompanying vegetable.

❑ Serves 4

75. Red Pumpkin Cutlets

The sweet flavour of red pumpkin is blended with
spices in which the cutlets are marinated.

INGREDIENTS

½ kg (18 oz) red pumpkin (kuddu or koru)

¾ teaspoon salt

1 teaspoon turmeric powder

¾ teaspoon chilli powder

1 cup dried breadcrumbs

4 eggs

Vegetable oil for frying

METHOD

1. Remove skin from piece of red pumpkin and slice pumpkin into thin slices ¼ cm ($^1/_8$-inch) thick (About 35 slices).

2. Mix together salt, turmeric powder and chilli powder and apply on all slices of pumpkin. Keep 1 hour.

3. Spread breadcrumbs on a flat surface (plate, chopping board or table) and press both sides of each slice of pumpkin into them gently. Dust off extra crumbs.

4. Separate eggs and beat egg whites till stiff. Blend in egg yolks and beat till well mixed.

5. In a frying pan, pour oil to a depth of 1 cm (½ inch). Heat to medium hot. Dip each slice of pumpkin in beaten egg and place gently in frying pan. Fry till golden on both sides and remove. Serve with mashed potatoes and boiled peas.

❑ Makes about 35 cutlets

76. Sweet Carrots

*The versatile carrot which is used with equally good effect
in pickles as well as sweets is cooked below as a sweetened vegetable.*

INGREDIENTS

½ kg (1 lb.) carrots

2 dessertspoons sugar

½ teaspoon salt

METHOD

1. Scrape and wash carrots, then cut them into fine strips 2½ cm to 4 cm (1 inch to 1½ inches) long.

2. Put carrots in pan, add water to just cover carrots, add salt and cook till carrots are tender.

3. Add sugar and continue cooking till water dries up.

4. Serve as an accompaniment to Brain Cutlets (p. 63) or Crumb-Fried Lamb Chops (p. 47).

77. Chora

Black-Eyed Beans

Black-eyed beans cooked with spices.

INGREDIENTS

1 cup chora (black-eyed beans)

1 onion, finely sliced

2 dried red Kashimiri chillies ⎤

6 large cloves garlic ⎥ Grind to
  (¾ teaspoon) ⎥ a paste*

1 teaspoon cumin seeds ⎦

1 cardamom, peeled ⎤

2 cloves ⎥ Powdered
  ⎥ coarsely
2 black peppercorns ⎦

1 teaspoon salt

2 tablespoons vegetable oil

METHOD

1. Soak chora in water overnight or at least 4 hours.

2. In a pan heat oil and fry onion in it till brown. Drain excess oil.

3. Add masala paste to the onion and cook 5 minutes. Add a little water if it becomes too dry.

4. Add cardamom, cloves and black peppercorns and cook 2 or 3 minutes more.

5. Drain water from chora and add chora to masala mixture. Add salt and blend all ingredients well.

6. Add 1 cup water, cover and cook on low heat till chora are cooked and soft. Add more water only if necessary, as no gravy is required.

7. Sprinkle with 1 dessertspoon chopped fresh coriander, 1 dessertspoon finely chopped onion and 1 finely chopped green chilli, before serving.

❑ Serves 4

* Or use 1 teaspoon Mangal's Red Chilli, Jeera And Garlic Paste.

78. Spicy Vegetable Stew

This spicy, sweet and sour vegetable stew is also called "Laganshala"
as it is often included in wedding lunches and dinners.

INGREDIENTS

½ kg (18 oz) sweet potatoes

¼ kg (9 oz) potatoes

¼ kg (9 oz) carrots

6 cherry tomatoes

¼ kg (2 medium) onions, finely sliced

8 cloves garlic

3 dried red Kashimiri chillies   } Grind to

1½ teaspoons cumin seeds   } a paste*

can use as base for other sauces

1½ cups water

2 teaspoons salt

1 tablespoon vinegar

1 tablespoon Worcestershire Sauce

1 tablespoon sugar

Vegetable oil as required

METHOD

1. Peel sweet potatoes and potatoes. Scrape and clean carrots.
2. Cut sweet potatoes, potatoes and carrots into tiny cubes.
3. In a "kadai", or bowl shaped vessel or deep frying pan, pour oil to a depth of 4 cm (1½ inches) and heat.
4. Fry cut vegetables separately in it and keep aside.
5. In a pan, fry the onions in 4 tablespoons oil till golden brown. Drain excess oil.
6. Add masala paste to onion and cook 5 minutes adding 1 tablespoon water, if it sticks to bottom of pan.
7. Add all the fried vegetables and mix well. Add salt and water and cook, covered, on low heat for 15 minutes.
8. Add cherry tomatoes and continue cooking till tomatoes are soft and the stew is almost dry. Add vinegar, Worcestershire Sauce and sugar and cook 5 to 10 minutes longer.
9. Serve as a separate vegetable dish or as an accompaniment to cutlets, chops or patties.

❑ Serves 4 to 6

   * Or use 1½ teaspoons Mangal's Red Chilli, Jeera And Garlic Paste.

79. Toorai Tamat

Toorai is a summer vegetable and among the variety of ways in which it can be cooked one of the tastiest is with tomato and spices.

INGREDIENTS

2 kg (4½ lbs) toorai, peeled and cut into thin round slices

2 large onions, finely sliced

2 large onions, finely chopped

4 large cloves garlic, finely sliced

1 cm (½ inch) piece of fresh ginger root, finely sliced

1 large tomato, chopped

2 teaspoons salt

2 teaspoons sugar

4 tablespoons vegetable oil

METHOD

1. Heat oil and fry sliced onion in it till golden coloured and soft. Drain excess oil.

2. Add garlic and ginger and fry 3 or 4 minutes.

3. Add tomato and blend well, then add toorai, chopped onion and salt. Bring to the boil, then lower heat and cook, uncovered, till toorai is tender and water has dried.

4. Add sugar and continue cooking a few minutes till sugar has dissolved.

5. Serve as an individual vegetable or as an accompaniment to mince, patties, cutlets or fried chops.

❑ Serves 4

80. Drumstick Akoori

Pulp of boiled drumsticks is cooked into an unusual mixture which makes an excellent savoury when served on toast.

INGREDIENTS

18 drumsticks

2 large onions, finely chopped

3 tablespoons finely chopped fresh coriander

2 green chillies, finely chopped

4 teaspoons gram flour (chickpea flour) or plain flour

$^2/_3$ teaspoon salt

3 tablespoons vegetable oil

METHOD

1. Cut each drumstick into 3 or 4 pieces and boil in water till tender.

2. Cut each piece down middle then remove pulp from inside. Discard skin.

3. In a pan, heat oil and fry onion in it till soft and pale gold, not brown.

4. Add coriander and chillies and cook 5 minutes.

5. Add drumstick pulp and salt and continue cooking 5 minutes more.

6. Add gram flour or plain flour and stir briskly for 2 or 3 minutes, then remove pan from heat.

7. Fry or toast 4 slices of bread, spread drumstick mixture evenly on each slice and serve.

❑ Serves 4

81. Chutney-Stuffed Bhindi (Okra)

Tender, large bhindi (okra), stuffed with chutney,
dipped in egg and crumbs and fried crisp.

INGREDIENTS

¼ kg (9 oz) large bhindi (okra)

3 tablespoons grated
fresh coconut or
desiccated coconut

3 dried red Kashimiri chillies

4 cloves garlic (½ teaspoon)

¼ teaspoon cumin seeds

} Grind to a paste to make chutney

½ teaspoon salt

1 egg, slightly beaten

½ cup dried breadcrumbs

Vegetable oil for frying

METHOD

1. Select large, tender bhindi (okra). Slit each bhindi down side but not completely. (The bhindi should not become 2 separate halves).

2. Add salt to chutney.

3. Stuff each bhindi with the chutney and try to bring the two edges together again.

4. Dip each bhindi in the beaten egg, then roll in breadcrumbs.

5. In a frying pan, pour oil to a depth of 1 cm (½ inch). Heat to medium hot and gently fry bhindi in it till cooked.

❑ Serves 3 to 4

Facing page—Akoori (page 100),
Overleaf—Eggs on Tomato (page 109)

82. Dal in Coconut Milk

An unusual way of cooking lentils.

INGREDIENTS

1 cup masoor dal (red lentils), soaked in water 1 hour

3 tablespoons vegetable oil

2 medium onions, finely sliced

3 dried red Kashimiri chillies ⎫
4 cloves garlic (½ teaspoon) ⎬ Grind to a paste*
1 teaspoon cumin seeds ⎭

1½ cups milk of ½ grated fresh coconut** (p. 16)

1½ teaspoons salt

1 tablespoon vinegar ⎫
1 tablespoon Worcestershire Sauce ⎬ Mix together in a bowl
¾ tablespoon sugar ⎭

METHOD

1. In a pan, heat oil and fry onion in it till golden brown. Drain excess oil.

2. Add masala paste and blend well, stirring gently. Cook for 3 minutes, adding 1 teaspoon water at a time if the masala tends to stick to bottom of pan.

3. Add 2 tablespoons water, simmer 1 minute then add dal and blend well.

4. Add salt and 2½ cups water and simmer, covered, till dal is three quarter cooked.

5. Add coconut milk and continue simmering till dal is well cooked and slightly thickened but still moist.

6. Mash dal through a strainer into another pan then add mixture of vinegar, sugar and Worcestershire Sauce and bring to the boil once before serving.

7. Sprinkle 2 teaspoons finely sliced fried onion and 2 teaspoons melted butter over the dal in the serving dish for added flavour.

❏ Serves 4

* Or use ¾ lightly packed teaspoon of Mangal's Red Chilli, Jeera And Garlic Paste.

** Or use 50 g (about 2 oz) Cream of Coconut with 1½ cups water, or use coconut powder (p. 19).

Previous page—Chutney Stuffed Brinjal (page 111),

Facing page—Chapat (page 134), Mumra Cheekee and Peanut Cheekee (page 139) and Kopra Pak (page 143)

83. Corn in Coconut Milk

A simple savoury.

INGREDIENTS

1 cup corn kernels

1 onion, finely sliced

¾ teaspoon salt

1 cup water

¾ cup coconut milk of ½ grated fresh coconut (p. 16)

2 tablespoons vegetable oil

METHOD

1. Heat oil and fry onion in it till soft and pale gold. Drain excess oil.

2. Add corn and mix well then add salt and water and cook, covered, on low heat till water has dried.

3. Add coconut milk and continue cooking till corn is soft and almost dry.

4. Serve as a savoury on fried slices of bread or as an accompaniment to cutlets and chops.

❑ 4 Servings

84. Masoor

Black lentils cooked in a very typical Parsi style.

INGREDIENTS

1 cup kala masoor (black lentils) soaked for 2 hours

1 onion, cut in half

100 gram (about ¼ lb) brinjal, (1 medium) cut into large pieces

2 onions, finely sliced

4 cloves garlic (½ teaspoon) ⎤
1 cm (½ inch) piece of fresh ginger root ⎟ Grind to a paste*
2 dried red Kashimiri chillies ⎟
1 teaspoon cumin seeds ⎦

1 cardamom, shelled ⎤
2 cloves ⎟ Pound together coarsely
3 black peppercorns ⎦

1 teaspoon Dhansak masala

1 teaspoon sugar

1 teaspoon vinegar

1 teaspoon salt

4 tablespoons vegetable oil

METHOD

1. Drain water from kala masoor, then boil kala masoor in 6 cups water with 1 onion cut in half, brinjal and salt. By the time the masoor are cooked all the water should be absorbed and the masoor grain should look whole, not mashy. Set aside. Or pressure cook with 2 cups water for 20 minutes.

2. Heat oil and fry sliced onion in it till golden. Remove half the onion and 2 tablespoons oil and keep aside.

3. Add masala paste to fried onion in pan and cook 5 minutes.

4. Add powdered spices and Dhansak masala and continue cooking 3 minutes longer.

5. Gently remove pieces of onion and brinjal from cooked masoor and mash the vegetables through a sieve into the masala mixture. Cook for 3 or 4 minutes till well blended.

6. Now add the masoor to the masala mixture, mix well, add sugar and vinegar and simmer, covered, for 10 minutes.

7. Remove to a serving dish and sprinkle reserved fried onion and oil over masoor.

❏ Serves 4

   * Or use 1 teaspoon Mangal's Red Chilli, Jeera And Garlic paste.

85. Fried Brinjal (Eggplant)

Slices of brinjal (eggplant or aubergine) marinated in a chilli mixture and fried.

INGREDIENTS

¼ kg (9 oz) brinjal (eggplant),
  cut in 1 cm (½ inch) rounds

1 teaspoon chilli powder

1 teaspoon salt } Combine in a bowl

¾ teaspoon turmeric powder

Vegetable oil for frying

METHOD

1. Rub chilli powder mixture on both sides of each slice of brinjal.

2. Place slices of brinjal in a plate and cover. Place a heavy weight on the cover so that it presses down on the brinjal and helps the water from the vegetable to come out.

3. Allow brinjal to marinate 1 hour. Pour away the liquid from the brinjal

4. Pour oil in a large frying pan to a depth of 1 cm (½ inch) and heat. When hot, fry slices of brinjal in it, turning them once so that both sides are slightly brown. Remove from pan and drain on paper towels. Serve with cutlets, chops, patties or gravied meat.

❑ Makes about 8 to 10 slices

86. Salnoo-Puri

Mildly spiced potatoes eaten with puris.

Salnoo

INGREDIENTS

½ kg potatoes, peeled and
  cut into 1 inch pieces

1 teaspoon mustard seeds

15 curry patta (curry leaves)

2 green chillies, finely chopped

½ teaspoon turmeric powder

2 tablespoons finely chopped fresh
  coriander

1¼ teaspoons salt

3 tablespoons vegetable oil

METHOD

1. Boil potatoes.

2. In a pan, heat oil and add mustard seeds.

3. Add curry patta and green chillies and cook 1 minute.

4. Add turmeric powder, salt, and potatoes and mix well. Add ¼ cup water, bring to the boil and cook 5 minutes, covered.

5. Add coriander and cook 2 minutes more. Remove from heat.

Puris

INGREDIENTS

1 cup wheat flour (atta)

¾ teaspoon salt

Oil for frying

METHOD

1. Sift flour and add salt.

2. Make into a medium hard dough with ½ cup to ¾ cup water and knead well for 10 to 15 minutes.

3. Cover and let stand at least 1 hour.

4. Divide dough in half. Sprinkle some flour on pastry board or table top and roll out dough into a large round ½ cm (less than ¼ inch) thick. Cut out puris with a cutter 6 cm (about 2½ inches) in diameter. Do the same with other half of dough.

5. Pour oil in a "kadai" or wok-shaped pan to a depth of 8 cm (3 inches) and heat to almost boiling.

6. Place one puri in it and press down on it with a flat, perforated spoon. This will help it to puff up. When golden brown, remove and fry another puri.

7. Fry all puris similarly and serve hot with potatoes.

❑ Serves 6

87. Carrot and Brinjal Bake

*Carrot and brinjal (eggplant or aubergine)
make an unusual but tasty combination.*

INGREDIENTS

750 g (1¾ lb) brinjal (eggplant),
  sliced into 1 cm (½ inch) rounds

250 g (9 oz) onion, coarsely chopped

250 g (9 oz) carrots, grated

¼ teaspoon chilli powder

2 dessertspoons sugar

6 dessertspoons tomato ketchup

Salt to taste

Vegetable oil as required

METHOD

1. In a large frying pan pour 4 tablespoons oil and heat. Place in the frying pan as many slices of brinjal as will fit and fry about 3 minutes on each side. Remove and keep aside. Add more oil if necessary and continue frying slices of brinjal till all have been fried.

2. In the same frying pan in 4 tablespoons oil fry onions till soft and pale yellow.

3. Add carrots, mix well and cook about 10 minutes till carrots are soft.

4. Add 1 cup water, chilli powder, sugar, tomato ketchup and 1½ teaspoons salt. Cook another 5 minutes, mixing all ingredients well.

5. In a deep, round baking dish cover bottom with slices of brinjal and sprinkle some salt over slices. Over these spread a layer of carrot mixture. Cover this with more slices of brinjal with a sprinkling of salt and carry on with alternate layers of carrot mixture and brinjal ending with carrot mixture for the topmost layer. Cover baking dish with a tight-fitting lid and bake in moderate oven 40 minutes.

❑ Serves 6

Desserts

Unlike as in Western cooking where a dessert forms an important part of a meal, when all diners look forward to a "happy ending" in the form of an exotic dessert, and some even ask what it is before beginning dinner, the repertoire of typical Parsi desserts is limited. Perhaps it is because of the sumptuous range of fare, that a meal usually ends with a simple dessert and many end it, instead, with a bite of "mithai" or sweetmeat.

However, "special-day" menus always include dessert which rounds off a meal in a most satisfying way.

88. Luggan Custard

A rich, baked pudding served traditionally at weddings.

INGREDIENTS

3 cups milk

3 semi-heaped dessertspoons sugar

125 g (4½ oz) white or yellow "pendas" (available from an Indian Sweetmeat shop) or 100 g cashewnuts, ground

2 eggs

½ teaspoon vanilla essence

1 dessertspoon charoli (a small nut, also called cherangia or chironji) or 1 desertspoon almonds blanched, skinned and finely sliced.

METHOD

1. Boil milk, adding 1 dessertspoon sugar and let simmer, uncovered, for 20 minutes. (Addition of sugar prevents milk from burning at bottom).

2. Add "pendas" or cashew nuts and remaining sugar and cook 5 to 10 minutes more, till sugar has dissolved.

3. Take pan off heat and allow to cool.

4. Separate eggs. Place egg whites in a deep bowl and beat with rotary beater till stiff.

5. Add yolks to whites and blend well.

6. Add vanilla essence to eggs.

7. Add cooled milk mixture to eggs and blend well.

8. Pour mixture into a baking dish, 10 inches by 8 inches, sprinkle with charoli or almonds and bake in moderate oven 45 minutes, or till top is nice and brown and the custard is firm.

❑ Serves 6

89. Sev

*Vermicelli, fried, cooked with sugar and topped with seedless raisins (kismis) and
almonds to be served as a sweet on days of celebration.*

INGREDIENTS

100 g (4 oz) very fine vermicelli

5 tablespoons oil

3 desertspoons sugar, or more according
to taste

2 tablespoons kismis (seedless raisins)

1 tablespoon almonds

1 teaspoon mixed cardamom and nutmeg
powder

1½ cups water, or as required

METHOD

1. In a deep pan, heat the oil.

2. Take pan off heat and add vermicelli and mix quickly till oil and vermicelli are well
   blended.

3. Place pan on medium heat and cook, stirring constantly for 5 minutes or until
   vermicelli is well fried and brown.

4. Add sugar and water to just cover vermicelli and cook, covered, on low heat for 5 to
   10 minutes, or until the vermicelli is soft and all the water absorbed.

5. Boil almonds in water 1 minute. Cool slightly, then remove skin and slice almonds very
   fine.

6. Fry almonds gently in a little oil or ghee in a frying pan for 1 or 2 minutes. Do not
   allow almonds to brown much. Remove and keep aside.

7. In the same oil or ghee fry the kismis for 1 or 2 minutes. Remove.

8. Place cooked vermicelli in serving dish, sprinkle with cardamom and nutmeg powder
   and top with fried almonds and kismis.

❏ Serves 4

90. Ravo

A sweet made of semolina traditionally served on festive occasions.

INGREDIENTS

2 dessertspoons melted butter or ghee

2 tablespoons semolina (sooji)

2 tablespoons sugar

2 cups milk

1 tablespoon seedless raisins (kismis)

¼ teaspoon mixed cardamom and nutmeg powder

15 almonds, blanched, skinned and finely sliced

METHOD

1. Heat butter or ghee and add semolina. Cook, stirring, till semolina is slightly fried and pale gold in colour.

2. Add sugar and milk and keep stirring till mixture thickens.

3. Pour into a shallow dish or pie plate and allow to cool and set.

4. Fry kismis in a little butter or ghee and remove when bloated. Fry almonds in same butter or ghee and remove before they change colour.

5. Sprinkle powdered cardamom and nutmeg, raisins and almonds over Ravo and serve.

❏ Serves 4

91. Doodh Pak Puri

A rich dessert made of sweetened milk, almonds and pistachios and accompanied by puris.

Doodh Pak

INGREDIENTS

1 litre milk (5 cups)

2 tablespoons cream

5 semi-heaped dessertspoons sugar

1 dessertspoon rice flour

4 cardamoms, shelled and roughly powdered

¼ teaspoon nutmeg powder

25 g (1 oz) almonds, blanched and thinly sliced

25 g (1 oz) pistachios, finely sliced

METHOD

1. Add 2 tablespoons milk to rice flour and make into a thin paste.

2. Put milk, sugar, cream and rice flour paste in a pan and bring to the boil.

3. Lower heat and allow milk to simmer, uncovered, till quantity is $^1/_3$ less and mixture has thickened. Stir occasionally to make sure mixture does not burn at the bottom.

4. Cool slightly, then add cardamom, nutmeg, almonds and pistachios.

5. Chill in refrigerator.

6. Serve cold with puris.

Puris

INGREDIENTS

1 cup all-purpose flour

1½ tablespoons vegetable oil or melted ghee

½ teaspoon salt

Approximately 4½ tablespoons water

Vegetable oil for deep frying

METHOD

1. Sift flour and salt.

2. Add 1½ tablespoons oil or ghee and blend well.

3. Knead, adding water gradually, to a soft dough so that dough springs back when pressed with finger. (Kneading will take about 10 minutes).

4. Cover and keep at least one hour.

5. Knead again for 2 or 3 minutes, then divide dough in half.

6. Roll one half into a big round almost ¼ cm ($^1/_8$ inch) thick and cut out as many puris as possible of about 5 cm (2 inches) diameter.

7. Do the same with other half of dough. Make a third round of left-over dough and cut more puris.

8. In a large "kadai" or wok-shaped pan, pour enough oil for deep frying and heat, but do not boil.

9. Place a few puris at a time in it and fry till they puff and become pale gold in colour. Keep ladling oil over puris as they rise to the surface as this will help them to puff up. Remove and keep aside.

10. Fry remaining puris the same way.

11. Serve with Doodh Pak.

❑ Serves 6

92. Chapat

These sweet pancakes can be served as a dessert and also with tea.

INGREDIENTS

3 eggs

4 dessertspoons sugar

¾ cup sifted all purpose flour

1½ dessertspoons semolina (sooji)

½ dessertspoon ghee or butter, melted and cooled

1 cup milk of ½ grated fresh coconut (p. 16)

12 almonds, blanched and skinned

½ teaspoon vanilla essence

Vegetable oil for frying

METHOD

1. Chop almonds very fine and keep aside.
2. In a pan put eggs and sugar and mix briskly with wooden spoon till sugar has melted.
3. Add flour and semolina and blend to a smooth paste.
4. Add melted butter or ghee and blend well.
5. Add coconut milk little by little mixing all the time till mixture resembles thick pancake batter. Add upto ¾ cup coconut milk and test mixture for thickness. Add remaining coconut milk only if necessary.
6. Add almonds and vanilla essence and blend well.
7. Keep mixture, covered, 1 to 1½ hours.
8. Heat a small 15 cm (6 inches) heavy-bottomed frying pan over medium heat and when hot pour ½ teaspoon oil into it and spread evenly over surface.
9. Pour 1 tablespoon mixture onto frying pan and quickly tilt it till it covers surface of pan.
10. Cook on low heat till one side is golden coloured then turn over and cook other side.
11. When both sides are cooked, remove pancake to a plate and fold in half, then fold again into quarter.
12. Smear surface of frying pan again with oil and continue making one pancake at a time till all the mixture has been used.
13. Serve warm, plain or with honey or golden syrup, as a dessert or with tea.

❑ Makes 8 to 10

93. Doodh Powva

A Sweet made of milk and flaked rice served ice cold as a dessert.

INGREDIENTS

2½ cups milk

¼ cup cream

3 tablespoons sugar

½ cup powva (flaked or pressed rice)

20 almonds, blanched, skinned and very finely sliced

15 pistachios, shelled, and very finely sliced

5 cardamoms, shelled and powdered (¼ teaspoon)

½ teaspoon powdered nutmeg

¾ teaspoon vanilla essence

METHOD

1. Clean and wash powva.

2. Give one boil to milk.

3. Remove ¼ cup milk and add to cream. Keep aside.

4. In rest of milk add sugar and cook till sugar is melted.

5. Give one more boil to milk then add powva and keep stirring till mixture is slightly thickened (about 15 minutes).

6. Add almonds and pistachios and simmer 5 minutes,

7. Remove from heat and when bubbling stops, add cream.

8. Cool, then add cardamom, nutmeg and vanilla. Mix well and refrigerate till required. Serve cold.

❑ Serves 6

Miscellaneous

From among the great variety of cookies and sweets, recipes of a few perennial favourites are given on the following pages.

Although much is available in the shops, ready-made, the tradition and satisfaction of home-cooking remains. The selection here includes recipes for cookies, sweets and tea-time eats which are easy to prepare and are more enjoyable when cooked at home.

94. Bhakra

Tea-time cookies

INGREDIENTS

1 tablespoon ghee (should be cool)

½ cup sugar

3 eggs

1 cup semolina (sooji or ravo)

$^2/_3$ cup all-purpose flour

½ cup wheat flour (atta)

1 teaspoon vanilla essence

¾ teaspoon baking powder

4 cardamoms, peeled and crushed

1 teaspoon nutmeg powder

2 tablespoons almonds, blanched, skinned and finely chopped

1 dessertspoon yoghurt

Vegetable oil for frying

METHOD

1. Sift separately semolina, all-purpose flour and wheat flour.

2. Put ghee and sugar in a deep pan and stir briskly with the hand, for 5 minutes, to lighten.

3. Add eggs, one by one and continue stirring briskly by hand till sugar has melted.

4. Add semolina to mixture and blend well.

5. Add all-purpose flour and continue mixing.

6. Add vanilla essence to mixture and mix all ingredients well.

7. Add baking powder, cardamom, nutmeg and almonds to wheat flour and blend well. Add to mixture and mix till all ingredients are well blended.

8. Add yoghurt and make into a soft, sticky dough. Cover and keep 3 to 4 hours.

9. Add about 1 tablespoon more wheat flour or semolina to the dough so that it is not too sticky.

10. Sprinkle a little wheat flour onto a pastry board or table top and roll out dough into a large round ½ centimeter (almost ¼ inch) thick.

11. Cut as many rounds of 6 centimeters diameter (about 2½ inches) as possible. Roll leftover dough into a big round again and once more cut small rounds from it. Continue this process till all the dough has been cut into small rounds.

12. In a "kadai" or wok-shaped pan, pour oil to a depth of 5 centimeters (2 inches) and heat. Deep fry bhakras in it on medium heat till golden brown.

13. Serve at once or cool and store in an air-tight jar.

❑ Makes about 24

95. Mumra Cheekee

A sweet of puffed rice and jaggery that goes well with a cup of tea.

INGREDIENTS

3 cups puffed rice (mumra)

110 g (4 oz) jaggery

1 dessertspoon lemon juice

METHOD

1. Place puffed rice in a moderate oven to make crisp.
2. In a pan, put the jaggery, broken roughly into small pieces, and melt over medium heat.
3. As soon as the jaggery thins add lemon juice and stir briskly.
4. Add puffed rice and continue stirring briskly, then quickly spread out mixture on an oiled marble-top table or in an oiled "thali" or tray. Quickly flatten mixture to 1 cm (½ inch) thickness by smoothing out with rolling pin or greased back of a bowl.
5. Allow to cool a few minutes, then cut into 5 cm (2 inches) squares and eat at once or store in air-tight jars (when completely cooled) for later use.

96. Peanut Cheekee

Use same method as for Mumra Cheekee except substitute 1 cup shelled, peeled, roasted peanuts for 3 cups puffed rice.

97. White Pumpkin Murumbo

A sweet pumpkin dish which may be served as an accompaniment with almost any dish or instead of jam at breakfast.

INGREDIENTS

1 kg (2¼ lbs) round white pumpkin

Sugar according to weight of pumpkin

10 cm (4 inches) cinnamon stick

¾ teaspoon mixed cardamom and nutmeg powder

METHOD

1. Peel pumpkin, remove seed section, then grate pumpkin.

2. Weigh grated pumpkin together with its water then weigh sugar equal to half the weight of pumpkin.

3. Put sugar, grated pumpkin and pumpkin water together with cinnamon stick in a large pan.

4. Place pan on medium heat and bring mixture to the boil. Lower heat, cover and cook 10 minutes.

5. Uncover pan and continue cooking on medium heat till all the liquid has just dried and pumpkin is golden brown. Do not overcook. Sprinkle cardamom and nutmeg powder and mix.

6. Cool thoroughly and store in air-tight jars. It keeps for several weeks. Refrigerate if necessary.

98. Ambakalya

A sweet mango dish which is a good accompaniment to
Dhansak or any other dal (lentil) dish.

INGREDIENTS

1 kg (2¼ lbs) small green mangoes
  (Choose slightly soft and ripened ones)

½ kg (18 0z) jaggery, roughly cut into
  small pieces. (Use little more if
  mangoes are very sour)

5 cm (2-inch) piece cinnamon stick

METHOD

1. Peel then cut each mango into 6 slices. Discard seeds.

2. Put mango slices in a pan, then cover and cook 5 minutes on medium heat, without adding any water, to slightly soften mangoes.

3. In another pan boil ¼ cup water and add jaggery. Cook till jaggery is melted.

4. Add mango slices and cinnamon stick to jaggery and cook, covered, on medium heat, 15 minutes.

5. Uncover and cook 10 to 15 minutes more till liquid becomes a medium thick syrup.

6. Cool before serving.

99. Falooda

A cool drink which is doubly delicious on hot days.

INGREDIENTS

1½ litres milk

200 g sugar (1 cup less 1 dessertspoon)

5 teaspoons tukmuri seeds soaked overnight in 1½ cups water

3 tablespoons rose syrup or ½ teaspoon rose essence or 2 dessertspoons rose water

1 heaped tablespoon cornflour (optional)

Vanilla ice cream or cream if desired

METHOD

1. Add sugar to milk and bring to the boil. Lower heat and simmer, uncovered, on very low heat 50 to 60 minutes.

2. Cool thoroughly.

3. Mix cornflour with 1½ cups water and cook on low heat till it begins to look transparent. Immediately pour mixture into a colander which should be placed over a pan containing ice and I cup water. Stir vigorously with the back of a round spoon or ladle till cornflour mixture passes through. It will fall into the iced water in drops and solidify. After ½ hour strain water.

4. To cooled milk, add rose syrup (if using rose essence or rose water add a few drops red food colouring to make pink Falooda). Also add tukmuri seeds and cornflour drops.

5. Chill in refrigerator.

6. Serve chilled in glasses and add a dessertspoon of vanilla icecream or 1 teaspoon cream per glass of Falooda, if desired.

❑ Makes 8 glasses

100. Kopra Pak

Coconut Fudge

INGREDIENTS

1 fresh coconut, grated

Sugar equal to 1½ times weight of grated coconut

2 tablespoons cream

½ teaspoon nutmeg and cardamom powder

One drop red food colour

½ to 1 teaspoon vanilla essence

½ teaspoon butter

METHOD

1. Grease a tray with butter.
2. In a pan, add grated coconut and sugar and place on medium heat. Blend well stirring constantly with wooden spoon, 2 minutes.
3. Add cream and blend well.
4. Cook, stirring continuously, till mixture leaves sides of pan and coats the spoon. Remove from heat.
5. Add vanilla essence and one drop of red food colour to give mixture a pale pink colour. Mix well.
6. Turn out into tray, sprinkle nutmeg and cardamom powder over surface and spread out mixture evenly to 1 cm (½ inch) thickness.
7. Cool 15 minutes, then mark into 3 cm (1½ inches) squares and allow to cool completely.
8. Break into pieces along marking lines. Store in airtight container.

101. Date Ghari

A rich date mixture is spread between pastry and fried.

INGREDIENTS

For Date Mixture

250 g (9 oz) dates, seeded

½ tablespoon ghee

2½ tablespoons sugar

½ teaspoon cardamom and nutmeg powder

½ teaspoon vanilla essence

For Pastry

¾ cup flour

½ teaspoon salt

¼ teaspoon baking powder

½ dessertspoon ghee

Vegetable oil for frying

METHOD

Date Mixture

1. Pass dates through mincing machine.

2. Heat ghee and add sugar.

3. When sugar has melted, add dates and cook till dates are fried and sticky and mixture is soft.

4. Add cardamom and nutmeg powder and vanilla essence. Blend well and allow mixture to cool.

Pastry

5. Sift flour, salt and baking powder. Add ghee and blend well.

6. Add gradually about 4 tablespoons water and make into a soft dough, kneading for 10 minutes. (When pressed with finger dough should spring back).

7. Divide dough and date mixture each into 5 portions.

8. Take one portion of dough and make into a small round of 7 cm (about 3 inches) in diameter.

9. Place one portion of date mixture in centre of round and spread out to 1 cm (½ inch) from edge of round. Turn the round into a ball pinching the edges together to seal in the date mixture.

10. Flatten ball gently and roll into thin round 11 cm (about 4½ inches) in diameter.

11. Do the same with remaining portions.

12. Pour oil in a frying pan to a depth of 2 cm (¾ inch) and heat to medium hot.

13. Place one ghari in it and fry gently till one side is golden brown. Ladle oil over the top while it is frying.

14. Turn over and fry till second side is golden brown. Remove from pan and fry others similarly.

15. Serve with tea.

❑ Makes 5

Glossary

Almonds	badam	Lentils	dal
Apricots	jurdaloo	Mint	phudina
Black eyed beans	chora	Mustard seeds	rai ka dana
Black peppercorns	kala miri	Nutmeg	jaiphal
Bombay Duck	Boomla	Okra	bhindi
Cardamom	elaichi	Papadum	papad
Carom seeds	ajwain or ajmo	Peanuts or groundnuts	moonghphali or sing
Cashewnuts	kaju	Pomfret	Chhumno
Cherangia	chironji or charoli	Poppy seeds	khus khus
Cinnamon	dalchini or tuj	Prawn	kolmi or jhinga
Clove	luvung	Red chilli	lal mirch
Coriander (fresh)	hara dhania or kothmir	Red pumpkin	kuddu or koru
		Saffron	kesar
Coriander seeds	dhania	Seer fish	Surmai
Cumin seeds	jeera	Sesame seeds	til seeds or tul
Curry leaves	curry patta	Semolina	sooji or ravo
Eggplant (brinjal)	baigan	Shrimp	kolmi or jhinga
Fenugreek seeds	methi	Spinach	bhaji
Flaked rice	powva	Sweet potato	kand or sukarkand
Garlic	lusun	Tamarind	imli or amli
Ghee	clarified butter	Turmeric	haldi
Ginger	adruk or adoo	Vermicelli	sevia or sev
Green chilli	hara mirch	Yam	kand or sukarkand
Indian Salmon	Rawas	Yoghurt	dahi
Jaggery	gur or gor